teaching strategies *in* **gifted education**

a
GIFTED CHILD TODAY
reader

teaching strategies *in* gifted education

edited by

susan k. johnsen

and

james kendrick

PRUFROCK PRESS, INC.

Library of Congress Cataloging-in-Publication Data

Teaching strategies in gifted education /
edited by Susan K. Johnsen and James Kendrick.
    p. cm.—(A gifted child today reader)
      ISBN 1-59363-170-7
      1. Gifted children—Education. I. Johnsen, Susan K. II. Kendrick, James,
    1974– III. Series.

    LC3993.T33 2005
    371.95'6—dc22

                                          2005019708

Printed in the United States of America.

ISBN 1-59363-170-7

At the time of this book's publication, all facts and figures cited are the most current available. All telephone numbers, addresses, and Web site URLs are accurate and active. All publications, organizations, Web sites, and other resources exist as described in the book, and all have been verified. The authors and Prufrock Press, Inc., make no warranty or guarantee concerning the information and materials given out by organizations or content found at Web sites, and we are not responsible for any changes that occur after this book's publication. If you find an error, please contact Prufrock Press, Inc.

Prufrock Press, Inc.
P.O. Box 8813
Waco, Texas 76714-8813
(800) 998-2208
Fax (800) 240-0333
http://www.prufrock.com

Contents

Overview   xi

Section I
Differentiation

1   A Template for a Differentiated Educational Program   3
    by Vicki Whibley

2   Modifying Regular Classroom Curricula   17
    for High-Ability Students
    by Laura McGrail

Section II
Teaching Strategies

3   Simulations: Active Learning for Gifted Students   27
    by Danna Garrison May

4   How to Use Thinking Skills to Differentiate Curricula   39
    for Gifted and Highly Creative Students
    by Andrew Johnson

5   Developing a Foundation   51
    for Independent Study
    by Steffi Pugh

6   The 2–5–8 Plan: Reaching All Children   65
    Through Differentiated Assessment
        by Laura Magner

7   Problem Solving and Gifted Education: 71
    A Differentiated Fantasy Unit
        by Kenneth Smith and Michele Weitz

Section III
Classroom Management

8   Cluster Grouping Elementary Gifted
    Students in the Regular Classroom: 83
    A Teacher's Perspective
        by Kevin M. Teno

9   The Room Meeting For G/T Students   97
    in an Inclusion Classroom
        by John Feldhusen and Hazel Feldhusen

10 Four Levels of Learning Centers   105
    for Use With Young Gifted Children
        by Peggy L. Snowden
        and Linda Garris Christian

11 Cooperative Learning: 119
    Abused and Overused?
        by Vickie Randall

Section IV
Dealing With Underachievement

12 Gifted Underachievement: 127
    Oxymoron or Educational Enigma?
        by Barbara Hoover-Schultz

13 Motivating the Gifted Underachiever: 137
    Implementing Reward Menus and Behavioral
    Contracts Within an Integrated Approach
        by Earl S. Hishinuma

14 Setting "Motivation Traps"   159
    for Underachieving Gifted Students
        by Donna Y. Ford, Sheila R. Alber,
        and William L. Heward

Section V
Professional Development
and School Improvement

15 Through the Looking Glass: One School's   171
    Reflections on Differentiation
        by Carol Tieso

16 What Gift? The Reality of the Student Who Is Gifted 183
    and Talented in Public School Classrooms
        by Tempus Fugit Glass

17 The Application of an Individual Professional   193
    Development Plan to Gifted Education
        by Frances A. Karnes and Elizabeth Shaunessy

About the Authors   203

Overview

*t*hese articles from *Gifted Child Today* were selected specifically for the teacher who is searching for teaching strategies to use with gifted students in the classroom. This overview provides a brief summary of the authors' major concepts covered in each of the chapters, including (a) characteristics of a differentiated curriculum, (b) specific instructional strategies, (c) methods for organizing and managing the environment for differentiation, (d) techniques for motivating underachieving gifted students, and (e) approaches for improving the school's gifted program using professional development.

In differentiating the regular classroom curriculum, the teacher modifies content, process, and product (Johnson). The content is the concepts and skills students are to learn, the process is the activities students use to learn the content, and the product is the evidence students show when they have learned the content. The content is frequently organized around conceptual themes and student interests (Whibley). It may be accelerated or enriched, depending upon each student's rate of learning (McGrail). Activities encourage the processes of higher levels of thinking (Johnson; Whibley) and independent research (Pugh; Whibley) and foster emotional, social, and ethical development (Whibley). Product assessment is ongoing and varied (Whibley), with students frequently selecting the method to show their understanding of the knowledge (Magner).

In teaching a differentiated curriculum, teachers frequently use specific strategies. Whether taught through questioning, directly, or with other instructional methods, most authors agree that differentiated activities must encourage higher level thinking (McGrail; Johnson; Magner; Pugh; Smith & Weltz; Whibley). Johnson views higher level thinking as a "cognitive process broken down into a set of explicit steps that are then used to guide thinking" (p. 24). These skills may be directly taught and then transferred to a content area, developed through content-related activities, or taught within a specific subject area (Johnson). For example, Smith and Weltz immerse complex thinking within a fantasy-based unit in which students learn about specific character traits and characteristics that are particular to the genre before solving open-ended problems. May uses simulations to stimulate critical and creative thinking and empathy for real-life decisions. Pugh develops higher order thinking and problem solving in an independent study course that is built upon individual student interest. Content knowledge is also aligned with higher order thinking in which students select levels of assessments that correspond to Bloom's Taxonomy (Magner).

In implementing a differentiated curriculum, authors recommend a variety of grouping arrangements and school or classroom management strategies. Teno suggests that gifted students be cluster grouped at a grade level and assigned to one classroom. This type of grouping allows students to receive all of their instruction within the regular classroom, with the gifted teacher serving as a resource to assist with curricular modifications and special projects. McGrail not only recommends cluster grouping, but also homogeneous cooperative groups so that students with similar abilities can interact with one another. Randall is particularly opposed to groups that are heterogeneous and involve cooperative learning because gifted students assume primary responsibility for other students' learning, do not acquire new knowledge, and are involved in activities that do not encourage higher order thinking.

Snowden and Christian view learning centers as an approach for managing differentiation with young gifted children. These centers may be teacher-planned/teacher-directed (i.e., traditional), teacher-planned/student-directed (i.e., discovery), student-planned/teacher-directed (i.e., teachable moments), and student-planned/student-directed (i.e., naturalistic). Solving classroom management problems is extended to students using class meetings (Feldhusen & Feldhusen). In this management model, students are involved in identifying problems and advancing solutions to improve learning in the classroom.

The authors also suggest schoolwide management strategies using Renzulli's total school improvement model (Tieso) or five service levels (Teno). The components of Renzulli's model include students interest, authentic methods, and real audiences (Whibley). Teno's five service levels are: Advocacy (identifying students in individualizing their programs); Special Opportunities (offering activities such as Math Olympiads); Extension of the Regular Curriculum (providing talent development and enrichment through the regular classroom); Modification of the Regular Curriculum (developing a plan for the gifted student within the regular classroom); and Pull-In Class (a special teacher working with gifted students in a separate classroom on projects related to their abilities and interests).

Gifted students who do not appear to be interested in a differentiated curriculum and exhibit low performance in the classroom have special needs and require different strategies (Ford, Alber, & Heward; Hishinuma; Hoover-Schultz). Some of these strategies include counseling, the Trifocal Model, an integrated systems approach, behavioral contracts, and motivating activities. The Trifocal Model is a comprehensive intervention that involves assessment, a focus on communication, changing expectations, identification, correction of deficiencies, and modifications at home and school (Hoover-Schultz). Hishinuma also describes a systems approach that incorporates comprehensive and ongoing assessment, teacher characteristics, curriculum and instruction, social/emotional development, school philosophy and procedures, parenting, and the home environment. More specific teaching strategies are establishing "motivation traps" such as units about heroes, projects based on a particular area of interest, classroom clubs, and activities that encourage social and emotional development such as pen pal clubs (Ford, Alber, & Heward).

Implementation of a quality differentiated curriculum depends on quality teachers. To address this challenge, Tieso, Glass, and Karnes and Shaunessy offer specific suggestions for professional development. Karnes and Shaunessy describe the design of an individual professional development plan in which teachers make decisions and set goals for improving their students' classroom performance. Tieso also involves teachers in their own development by using peer coaching. Glass explains the specific areas that a gifted specialist should possess: content sophistication, the ability to differentiate lessons and units, and the skill to teach complex ideas.

We want to thank these authors for their contributions. We hope these articles assist you in effectively teaching a differentiated curriculum to gifted students.

Susan K. Johnsen
James Kendrick
Editors

Differentiation

~

chapter 1

A Template for a Differentiated Educational Program

by **Vicki Whibley**

*t*he following is an excerpt from a play in which each character uses one of de Bono's (1999) Six Thinking Hats. Readers might quickly recognize the positive thinker, the black hat thinker, and the reaction thinker.

ALICE ROBINSON (NURSE): No! Please don't close down the bath house. I'll lose my job and home because I'd be so poor. My children and I would live on the streets. Please, no!

NEIL (CARETAKER): This place won't last much longer if it is kept as a bath house. It's a maintenance nightmare! I'm sure you already know that iron rusts, wood rots, and stone crumbles under the action of the strong hydrogen sulfide acid with which the waters are charged! When are the repairs going to end?

DR. JOHN WHITE: We've heard a lot of negative points about keeping the bath house and a few positive ones. What about some more positive points?

DR. ALICE BLAIR (BALNEOLOGIST): I agree with my predecessor, Dr. Doris Duncan. We should continue with the bath house, as it can provide miraculous cures. It is complementary to modern medicine.

This play was written and produced by two gifted 10-year-old children, and it is the result of a differentiated educational program.

In New Zealand, it is common to provide servicesfor gifted children in the regular classroom. But, in a busy classroom, how can we, as educators, provide for the special needs of these children? A differentiated educational program (DEP) is often required for children who demonstrate exceptional ability when compared to their peers. The purpose of a DEP is to provide a holistic educational experience relevant to the students' special needs. The key word is *differentiated*, since gifted children require learning tasks that match their particular cognitive and affective characteristics. The template was created for use by two gifted children (see Figure 1.1). I've since found this template to be adaptable to a variety of topic studies and conceptual themes that interest gifted children. This chapter provides a practical example and identifies curriculum models, type of content, implementation strategies, and evaluation pointers.

Curriculum Models

Two curriculum models, REACH (Cathcart, 1994) and the Individualized Educational Programs Model (Renzulli & Smith, 1979), form the basis for the DEP template, providing a framework and ensuring that the DEP is defensible and educationally sound for gifted children. The REACH model for teaching gifted children, which was developed in New Zealand, works from the basic premise that gifted and talented children need a structured program to meet their specific learning needs. The establishment of an environment in which children can demonstrate their abilities is a prerequisite. There are four components that together form this holistic model:

1. Generate a high level of interest.
2. Develop the skills of research, observation, communication, and thinking.
3. Develop children's intellectual and creative potential.
4. Foster emotional, social, and ethical development.

The second model chosen is based on the Enrichment Triad Model (Renzulli, 1977). It serves as a guide for Type III enrichment, which consists of individual or small-group investigations of real-life problems that emulate the methodological processes adults use in the same field of endeavor. Components of this model include interest, authentic methods, and real audiences.

The goals of the DEP include the four components of REACH and incorporate some of Renzulli's ideas.

Interest

To achieve a high level of interest, Sewell (1996) suggested that "the children's ideas for study are often more relevant and destined for greater success than teacher initiated topics" (p. 230). Since Renzulli and Smith (1979) cautioned that care should be made not to push children into anything in which they show only slight interest, two other program components are included: appropriate audiences for student products and adequate resources. A wide variety of resources are used, including written material, artifacts, people, and resources created by the children.

Thinking Skills

It is also important to provide opportunities for children to develop the skills of research, observation, communication, and thinking in a meaningful context. Renzulli (1977) and Borland (1989) wrote of their concern about gifted programs becoming merely a collection of exercises taught in isolation. Instructional strategies such as brainstorming encourage creativity and critical thinking, but should be used with quality content that is interesting and complex. For example, DOVE rules and SCAMPER prompters (Fogarty, 1991) are acronyms that encourage children to substitute, combine, adapt, and modify ideas and "hitchhike" on each other's thoughts to achieve vast numbers of ideas when

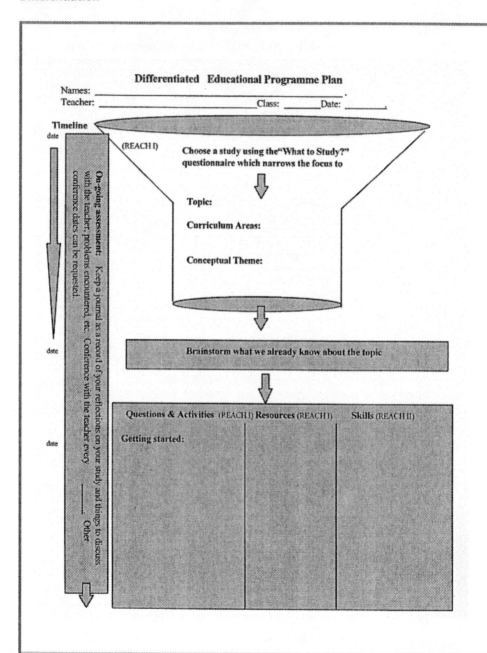

Figure 1.1. **Differentiated educational**

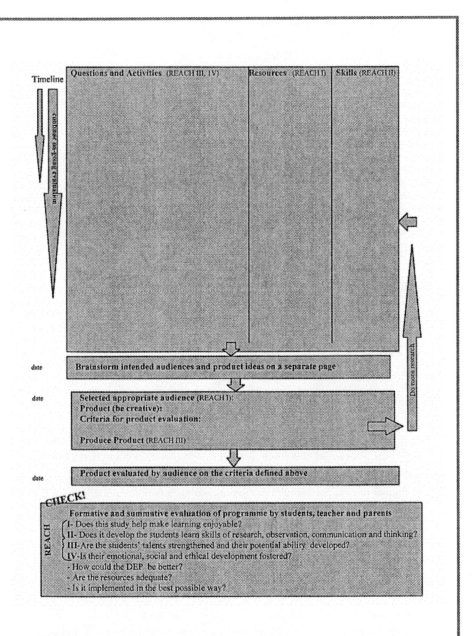

Timeline

continue one-going evaluation

Do more research

Questions and Activities (REACH III, IV) | **Resources** (REACH I) | **Skills** (REACH II)

date — Brainstorm intended audiences and product ideas on a separate page

date — Selected appropriate audience (REACH I):
Product (be creative):
Criteria for product evaluation:

Produce Product (REACH III)

date — Product evaluated by audience on the criteria defined above

CHECK!

REACH

Formative and summative evaluation of programme by students, teacher and parents
I- Does this study help make learning enjoyable?
II- Does it develop the students learn skills of research, observation, communication and thinking?
III-Are the students' talents strengthened and their potential ability developed?
IV-Is their emotional, social and ethical development fostered?
- How could the DEP be better?
- Are the resources adequate?
- Is it implemented in the best possible way?

program planning template

brainstorming (see Figures 1.2 and 1.3).

de Bono's Six Thinking Hats and PMI (Pluses, Minuses, and Interesting Points) strategies enable children to make highly informed judgments (de Bono, 1973, 1999). These two strategies encourage the children to think beyond their obvious initial responses to consider other perspectives on issues. de Bono's Six Thinking Hats include:

Defer judgment.

Opt for original and off-beat.

Vast numbers are important.

Expand on ideas by hitchhiking.

Figure 1.2. **DOVE rules for brainstorming**

1. White Hat—Information: What are the facts?
2. Red Hat—Feelings: What do I feel about this?
3. Black Hat—Judgment: What is wrong with this?
4. Yellow Hat—Benefits: What are the good points?
5. Blue Hat—Thinking: What hat should be used next?
6. Green Hat—Creativity: What new ideas are possible?

Intellectual and Creative Activities

To ensure that a DEP involves the complex and abstract thinking required of a truly differentiated program for gifted children, Bloom's (1956) taxonomy can be used as a checking tool. It should *not* be used as a structure in which a box for each level of the taxonomy has to be filled with an activity, which only fractionates learning. A purposeful study using the methodology of the relevant field (e.g., historical research or scientific investigation) enables higher order thinking skills to take place naturally.

Depth of content can be attained by studying or researching concepts in natural and "authentic" situations (Le Sueur, 1986). For example, instead of reading about general environmental issues, focus students' attention on problems with the local landfill. Likewise, observing ants in their natural habitat is more useful than briefly and broadly studying insects. An in-depth study on ants would include creating a classroom terrarium and observing the ants' behavior, environment, diet, and movement.

Substitute:	Who else instead? What else instead? Other ingredient? Other material? Other process? Other power? Other place? Other approach? Other tone of voice?
Combine:	How about a blend, an assortment, an ensemble? Combine units? Combine purposes? Combine appeals? Combine ideas?
Adapt:	What else is like this? What other idea does this suggest? Does something in the past offer a parallel? What could I copy? Whom could I emulate?
Modify:	New twist? Change meaning, color, motion, sound, order, form, shape?
Magnify:	What to add? More time? Greater frequency? Stronger? Higher? Longer? Thicker? Extra value? Add ingredient? Duplicate? Multiply? Exaggerate?
Minify:	Smaller? Condensed? Miniature? Lower? Shorter? Lighter? Split up? Understate?
Put to other uses:	New ways to use as is? Other uses if modified?
Eliminate:	Omit? What to subtract?
Reverse:	How about opposites? Turn it backward? Turn it upside down? Reverse roles? Change shoes? Turn tables? Turn the other cheek?
Rearrange:	Interchange components? Other patterns? Other layout? Other sequence? Transpose cause and effect? Change pace? Change schedule?

Figure 1.3. SCAMPER

Note. Adapted from *SCAMPER: Games for Imagination Development* (p. 6), by B. Eberle, 1996, Waco, TX: Prufrock Press. Copyright ©1996 by Prufrock Press. Adapted with permission.

Relating content to a conceptual theme also enables an in-depth study (Riley, 1997). This method is valuable because it draws on gifted children's curiosity and ability to see relationships. In particular, it is a useful holistic approach when the same DEP caters to a group of children whose strengths are in different curricular areas. Some ideas for conceptual themes are change, adventure, mystery, power, and survival.

Emotional, Social, and Ethical Development

By fostering emotional, social, and ethical development, Cathcart (1994) meant "putting learning into the context of human experience and supporting children in their growth toward a caring concern for others" (p. 148). Along with the creation of a product, questions and activities can encourage evaluation involving ethical and emotional awareness. For example, in the bath house study described below, the children were required to use PMIs and the Six Thinking Hats to evaluate whether the bath house should be closed. This involved the consideration of ethical issues such as whether tourists should have been concerned about sharing the thermal waters with patients and whether it is right for the bath house to close down for financial reasons when it was providing a useful service.

Social development occurs through the skills required to develop a relationship with a mentor. This relationship involves sharing a common interest with a more experienced person. In the bath house study, a local historian shared his knowledge with the children in a more involved manner than a usual resource person—he helped guide the students in their research. The students developed socially through cooperating with one another and through interviewing resource people. Students had to practice politeness and etiquette when asking for help.

According to Cathcart (1994), if social, emotional, and ethical growth is to occur, then the children need to have self-knowledge. Just being in a differentiated education program, children recognize that they do have special abilities. They assess themselves when planning their program and reflect about their performance in a journal. This assessment provides information that enables students to develop self-knowledge.

Implementation

The regular classroom is a convenient base for implementing a differentiated educational program. It has the advantages of a teacher with holistic knowledge of children, opportunities for informal assessment, and a flexible timeline. However, while using the classroom as a base, it is important to take the study beyond the classroom walls. Clark (1992) claimed that this extension enabled natural and integrated learning. Sewell (1996) agreed: "genuine issues, problems, and people in the local community are a valuable and often underutilized resource for gifted children" (p. 230). An audience for student products needs to be organized from the wider community, rather than relying on captured classroom peers who may not be an appropriate audience (Renzulli & Smith, 1979).

The significant roles involved in a DEP are that of the mentor, parents, children, and teacher. A mentor is needed to help children with the methodological process and to share his or her passion for the topic. Parents need to be informed so that they can support their children with homework. Children need to share the responsibility of learning and evaluation, including self-assessment. The teacher is a facilitator and advisor. The teacher has three major responsibilities for guiding these types of differentiated learning experiences (Renzulli, 1977):

1. Provide strategies for identifying and focusing student interests.
2. Find appropriate outlets for student products.
3. Provide an appropriate environment (used in a wide sense).

Key teacher attributes are enthusiasm and willingness to explore new avenues while learning alongside the children.

Evaluation

There needs to be evaluation of the DEP itself and evaluation of the children's achievements, as well as open communication between the teacher and others involved. Questions need to be asked again and again throughout all the stages of the DEP. For example, the teacher doesn't want to discover at the conclusion that the resources were inadequate or the children weren't interested. Something should have been done about these weaknesses earlier. The evaluation questions on the template are not a comprehensive list (see Figure 1.1); there are many more that could be asked depending on the particular purpose or the audience.

Assessing whether children have achieved their objectives is part of evaluating the success of a DEP. A journal, which can be a combination of a log book, diary, and goal-setting record, is an effective device to see how children are coping with the DEP. It encourages children to reflect on their own learning by recording their reactions and responses to what they have read and stating problems they encounter. Conferencing is another means of formative evaluation. When conferencing, the teacher is supporting children and looking for depth of learning. Teacher questions need to encourage the children to clarify, probe, and analyze perspectives, implications, and consequences. Evaluation of the children's products is another means to assess achievement. Note that specific criteria need to be developed prior to production.

Bridging Theory and Practice: A Practical Example

The following DEP design was first piloted using the topic of the bath house, a significant local historical building. It was originally a bath house, then it was closed and later converted to a museum. Since it is located in a thermal area, its future for storing museum collections is being reevaluated. Two children chose the topic based on their strengths in the subjects of history, language, and science. The major generalizations from each field were integrated around the conceptual theme of "change."

After choosing the topic and brainstorming what they already knew, the children generated their own questions (see Figure 1.4). The questions naturally lent themselves to using a variety of resources and developing a range of skills in research, observation, communication, and thinking. The children visited the bath house several times to observe closely some of the old baths and other artifacts such as plumbing and old clocks. They were fascinated with the love bath and the price board of different treatments available in the women's "new" Priest Bath.

Back in the classroom, the children gathered a variety of resources to make a learning center. It was successful in attracting the interest of other class members, who requested to be in

Questions (REACH I)	Activities (REACH I, III, IV)	Skills (REACH II)	Resources (REACH I)
What caused the bath house to be built? Was there a debate about it like the current casino debate?	• identify the influences (e.g., who was involved, time period, other bath houses in the world) • create a learning center in the classroom • bring photos to "life" by inventing dialogue and imagining with all the senses (Sewell, 1996) • visit the bath house and take photos	• research—weeding/selecting information • observations (e.g., of building and of foreground and background, similarities and differences in photos)	• librarians and museum staff • books • each other's contributions to the learning center and glossary • photos, prints, pictures, sketches • newspaper clippings, encyclopedia, atlases
Why did the bath house close?	• add to the learning center • identify the historical figures involved in the closure • do a role-play debating whether it should close where each character is a historical figure with an appropriate one of the "Six Thinking Hats"	• synthesizing the information gathered • analysis using the Six Thinking Hats • role-playing	• books and old newspaper articles • previous staff of the bath house and recordings of their comments • the building itself and artifacts such as old equipment, baths, uniforms • local historian and possible mentor
Do we think the bath house should have closed?	• interview a doctor about current medical knowledge on spa treatments and compare it to the views of balenologists in the past • research about how other bath houses in the world have fared • discuss whether it is right for the bath house to close down for financial reasons when it provided a service (note link to current hospital closures) • discuss whether tourists should have been concerned about sharing the thermal water with patients	• interviewing—questioning skills • comparisons • evaluating—using the Six Thinking Hats and PMIs	• de Bono resources on thinking skills • Encarta CD-ROM • tourist brochures • children's own opinions on ethical issues • currently practicing doctor
What are some ideas for the future use of the building?	• find out what the public, current staff, and tourists think on the future use of the building • rank whose needs are most important: locals, tourists, or workers • discuss if the building should remain in its own right for aesthetic reasons only • do a PMI on each idea on the future use of the building	• interviewing, brainstorming using DOVE rules and SCAMPER techniques • creativity • evaluating using PMI technique • ranking • discussing *Note: other skills are the conference and negotiating skills used by the teacher	• the building itself • museum staff, public, tourists • charts of DOVE rules and SCAMPER techniques

Figure 1.4. **Content of the bath house study**

the play or contribute bits and pieces to the display, with one class member contributing a painting of a room at the bath house. The learning center also included old and recent student photographs, a pamphlet on an Irish bath house, a glossary, books, photocopied newspaper articles, and some fake plumbing made of rolled paper with the sign: "Do not spit in the baths!"

The children then had to synthesize their information to create a product. After brainstorming many product ideas (see Figure 1.5), they chose to write a play and videotape the performance. They also chose to produce a teacher resource kit for use in local schools. Criteria for the evaluation of these products were identified before the children produced them. For example, it was decided that teachers would be asked to rate the kit according to its factual information, user-friendliness, attractiveness, and originality.

Evaluation occurred throughout all stages. During the ongoing evaluation, the teacher noted that a tighter time frame than the one originally negotiated by the children was required and that the children needed more class time to pursue their studies. At the initial planning stage, the teacher also determined the degree to which higher thinking skills and the four components of the REACH model were included in the student-generated questions and related activities. It was found that the learning tasks were well differentiated, as average students would have struggled with the task commitment required for this in-depth study of the bath house. The learning also matched the students' interests and abilities. One student's enthusiasm was evidenced by her frequently asking during other classroom work, "When can we carry on with the bath house study?" Consequently, the students (and the teacher) were able to answer "yes" to the most important evaluation question: "Do we enjoy learning?"

This evaluation question is the whole point of providing a DEP (Borland, 1989). Teachers should enable their children to explore new avenues by trying out this template using a topic initiated by the children. This DEP template provides the framework for a defensible holistic educational program that builds on children's strengths and meets their learning needs to ensure their love of learning. Its adaptable nature can provide many enjoyable learning experiences for gifted children.

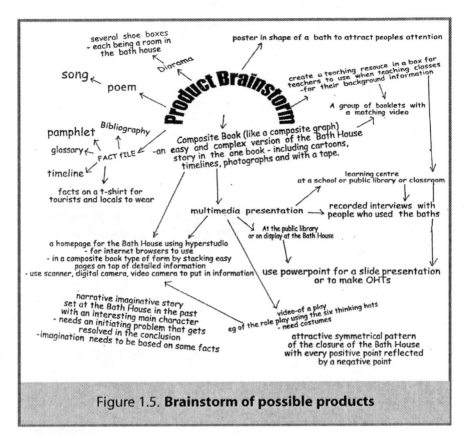

Figure 1.5. **Brainstorm of possible products**

References

Borland, J. H. (1989). *Planning and implementing programs for the gifted*. New York: Teachers College Press.

Bloom, B. S. (Ed.). (1956). *Taxonomy of educational objectives: The classification of educational goals. Handbook I: The cognitive domain*. New York: Longmans, Green.

Cathcart, R. (1994). *They're not bringing my brain out*. Auckland, New Zealand: REACH Publications.

Clark, B. (1992). *Growing up gifted: Developing the potential of children at home and at school* (4th ed.). New York: Macmillan.

de Bono, E. (1973). *CoRT 1: Teachers Handbook*. Oxford, England: Pergamon Press.

de Bono, E. (1999). *Six thinking hats* (Rev ed.). New York: Back Bay Books.

Fogarty, R. (1991). *Keep them thinking*. Moorabbin, Victoria, Australia: Hawker Brownlow Education.

Le Sueur, E. (1986). Educational provisions: Primary schools. In D. McAlpine & R. Moltzen (Eds.). *Gifted and talented: New Zealand perspectives* (pp. 159–169). Palmerston North, New Zealand: ERDC Press.

Renzulli, J. S. (1977). *The enrichment triad model: A guide for developing defensible programs for the gifted and talented.* Mansfield Center, CT: Creative Learning Press.

Renzulli, J. S., & Smith, L.H. (1979). *A guidebook for developing individualized educational programs (IEP) for gifted and talented children.* Mansfield Center, CT: Creative Learning Press.

Riley, T. (1997). Tools for discovery: Conceptual themes in the classroom. *Gifted Child Today, 20*(1), 30–33, 50.

Sewell, A. (1996). Social studies. In D. McAlpine & R. Moltzen (Eds.), *Gifted and talented: New Zealand perspectives* (pp. 219–232). Palmerston North, New Zealand: ERDC Press.

Author Note

Credit is given to Nicola McHaffie and Zara Kinzett for their help in developing the template. It was their idea to use a flow chart.

chapter 2

Modifying Regular Classroom Curricula for High-Ability Students

by **Laura McGrail**

any educators have become well-versed in modifying the regular classroom curriculum to meet the needs of students with disabilities. Educators are not as experienced, however, in meeting the instructional needs of high-ability students. In a growing number of states, revisions in regulations pertaining to gifted and talented students are requiring that high-ability students, previously served in part-time pull-out programs, must also receive appropriate instruction within the context of their regular classrooms. For example, in Kentucky, high-ability students can no longer be viewed as sufficiently served by a once-monthly or once-weekly program. These students have educational needs that must be met daily, just as students with disabilities have.

Many regular education teachers report that meeting the needs of high-ability students equals and often exceeds the challenges of integrating disabled students in their classrooms. High-ability students can be delightful, but they can also be demanding, impatient, perfectionistic, sarcastic, and disruptive. In addition, few regular education teachers have received sufficient training in issues related to gifted and talented education. Before teachers can develop appropriate instructional strategies to meet the needs of high-ability students, they must recognize the value of such efforts. For many educators, services to gifted and talented students may seem to be elitist. However, public education is founded on the belief that all students (including those with high abilities) have the right to instruction appropriate to their needs. Gifted and talented students, like all students, should learn something new every day.

General Strategies for Modifying the Curriculum

The objectives for modifying standard curricula for high-ability students include

- meeting the learning capacity of the students,
- meeting the students' rapid rates of learning in all or some areas of study, and
- providing time and resources so that students can pursue areas of special interest.

In order to modify standard curricula for high-ability students, Lois Roets (1993) proposed three options:

- lesson modifications,
- assignment modifications, and
- scheduling modifications.

Lessons can be modified through acceleration or enrichment of content. Assignments can be modified through reducing regular classroom work or providing alternate assignments. Scheduling options include providing opportunities for high-ability students to work individually through independent study, share learning in homogeneous groupings with peers of similar ability and interests, and participate in heterogeneous groupings of mixed-ability students.

Lesson Modifications

One way teachers can extend or enrich the content they present is by asking open-ended questions. Such questions stimulate higher order thinking skills and give students opportunities to consider and express personal opinions. Open-ended questions require such thinking skills as comparison, synthesis, insight, judgment, hypothesis, conjecture, and assimilation. Such questions can also increase student awareness of current events. Open-ended questions should be included in both class discussions and assignments. They can also be used as stimulation for the opening or conclusion of a lesson.

Another strategy for lesson modification developed by Susan Winebrenner (1992) is to use Bloom's taxonomy of six levels of thinking to develop lesson content. Bloom's model implies that the "lower" levels (knowledge, comprehension, and application) require more literal and less complex thinking than the "higher" levels (analysis, evaluation, and synthesis). Teachers are encouraged to develop thematic units with activities for students at all ability levels. This strategy involves four steps. Teachers first choose a theme that can incorporate learning objectives from several different subject areas. Secondly, teachers identify 6 to 10 key concepts or instructional objectives. Third, they determine which learner outcomes or grade-level competencies will be targeted for the unit. Finally, they design instructional activities to cover each of the six levels of thinking.

Assignment Modifications

High-ability students are often expected to complete assignments that they find boring or irrelevant because they represent no new learning for them. Allowing them to reduce or skip standard assignments in order to acquire time to pursue alternate assignments or independent projects is called compacting. The curriculum for a gifted student should be compacted in those areas that represent his or her strengths. When students "buy time" for enrichment or alternate activities, they should use that time to capitalize on their strengths, rather than to improve skills in weaker subjects. For example, a student advanced in math should have a compacted curriculum in that area with opportunities given for enriched study in mathematics.

The first step in compacting the curriculum is determining the need to do so. A student is a candidate for compacting if he or she regularly finishes assignments quickly and correctly, consistently scores high on tests related to the modified area, or demonstrates high ability through individualized assessment, but not daily classwork (i.e., he or she is gifted, but unmotivated for the standard curriculum).

The second step in compacting the curriculum is to create a written plan outlining which, if any, regular assignments will be completed and what alternate activities will be accomplished. A time frame for the plan should also be determined. Modification plans can be limited to a few days (i.e., length of lesson or chapter) or extend over the course of an entire school year.

Alternate assignments for high-ability students can either be projects related to the modified area of study that extend the curriculum, or they can be independent projects that are chosen based on students' individual interests. Winebrenner (1992) described a strategy in which students use written independent study contracts to research topics of interest to become "resident experts." The students and teacher decide upon a description and the criteria for evaluating each project. A deadline is determined, and by that date, each student must share his or her project with the entire class. Before choosing their projects, students are also given time to "browse." After completing compacted work, students are allowed to look through research materials to explore various topics. A deadline for choosing a topic for independent projects is also given to the students to limit their browsing time.

Scheduling Modifications

Cooperative learning through traditional heterogeneous groups is often counterproductive for high-ability students. When the learning task involves a great deal of drill and practice, these students often end up doing more teaching than learning. When placed in homogeneous cooperative learning groups, however, gifted students can derive significant learning benefits. This does not mean that high-ability students should never participate in heterogeneous cooperative learning groups. Rather, groupings should be chosen based on the task that is being assigned. When the task includes drill and practice, such as math computation or answering comprehension questions about a novel, gifted students should be grouped together and given a more complex task. When the task includes critical thinking, gifted students should be part of heterogeneous groups to stimulate discussions. Open-ended activities are excellent choices for heterogeneous groupings.

Cluster grouping of high-ability students into the same classroom is another option for meeting the needs of gifted students in the regular classroom. The traditional method of assigning students to classes has often been to divide the high-ability students "equally" among the available classes so each teacher would have his or her "fair share." Under this system, however, each teacher must develop strategies for modifying the curriculum to meet the needs of the advanced students. With cluster grouping, four to six high-ability students are placed in the same classroom. This system allows the students to learn with and from each other and reduces the need for multiple teachers to develop appropriate instructional modifications.

Case Studies

The following case studies describe how the curriculum was modified for three academically able students.

Mark

Mark entered first grade reading at a fourth-grade level. He had mastered math concepts that challenged his first-grade peers. He was placed in a second-grade class for math instruction and in a third-grade class for reading and spelling instruction. Despite these opportunities, Mark was always the first to finish assignments and spent the majority of his school day reading library books or playing computer games. His parents and teacher were concerned that he was not sufficiently challenged, but as a 6-year-old, he was too young to participate in the district's pull-out gifted program. They were also concerned that he was having difficulty developing friendships in his classroom since he spent much of the day apart from his homeroom peers. A request for consultation was made to the school psychologist.

With input from Mark's parents and teachers, an independent study contract was developed for Mark to channel his high reading abilities toward study in a specific area. After browsing for a week, he chose dinosaurs as his project area. Mark then narrowed his focus to the Jurassic Period and decided to create a classroom reference book complete with pictures he drew. When he completed his daily work, Mark researched his topic area and worked on his project. When completed, Mark's teacher asked him to share his project with his classmates. Because he had chosen a topic of high interest to his peers, Mark's status as "resident expert" on dinosaurs made him attractive to his classmates. Mark's teacher encouraged these budding friendships by asking the other students to bring dinosaur toys and books from home to share with the class during the following weeks.

Katrina

Katrina's parents chose to move her from a private school to public school at the end of her third-grade year. Following the advice of the private school staff, Katrina's parents enrolled her in a second year of third grade at the public school due to reported weaknesses in reading and written expression. After a few weeks of school, Katrina's teacher approached the school psychologist with her concern that retention may not have been in Katrina's best interest. The teacher reported that Katrina was performing on grade level in all areas and demonstrated high-ability math skills.

Upon meeting with Katrina's parents, however, they expressed the desire to keep her in the third grade. They felt that Katrina had suffered no harmful effects from the retention since it involved a move to a new school with different peers. Further, Katrina's parents reported that she felt very comfortable and successful in her classroom. Although the committee decided to keep Katrina in the third grade, they developed a compacted curriculum for her in the area of math. A contract was written specifying modifications for Katrina in the regular class math curriculum. She was required to complete half of the assignments given to her peers, as long as she did so with 90% or higher accuracy. When finished with her modified assignment, Katrina then used her time earned through compacting for enriched study in mathematics. The committee was careful to avoid presenting material to Katrina that she would study in the future to avoid the possibility of repetition. Instead, an enriched program of study was developed that emphasized critical thinking and problem solving related to the addition and subtraction being taught in her classroom.

Katrina's contract included several choices of activities, any of which she could choose to do on a given day, such as creating story problems for the class to solve, drawing pictures or using manipulatives to demonstrate calculation problems, or activities involving measuring, classifying, estimating, and graphing. Katrina's teacher would present a specific activity choice in these areas that extended and enriched the basic concepts being taught to the class as a whole.

With these modifications, Katrina's advanced skills in math were addressed. Her parents and teacher judged her school year a success, and Katrina made an easy transition to fourth grade, where she was able to work on grade-level material with an average level of accuracy in all areas.

Adam

Adam demonstrated a very high spoken vocabulary and advanced ideas when participating in class. He completed few of his assignments, though, and showed strong resistance to putting pencil to paper despite obvious high abilities. He was able to read orally at a level 2 years above his fourth-grade status and could perform multidigit calculation problems mentally. However, in the classroom, Adam demonstrated many task avoidance and disruptive behaviors. His teacher and parents were frustrated by his lack of work output and behavior problems, and they sought assistance from the school psychologist.

In interviewing Adam, the psychologist found that he did not see the need to put on paper answers he already knew. It seemed likely that Adam's behavior problems were related to boredom and frustration. To test this theory, the psychologist recommended the use of Winebrenner's (1992) "Most Difficult First" strategy. With this strategy, the teacher identifies the most difficult portion of an assignment and the student is allowed to attempt that portion of the assignment first. If he or she completes it with 100% accuracy, the student is excused from the remainder of the assignment and allowed to use his or her free time to pursue an alternate activity.

Adam was resistant to this strategy at first, but he quickly saw its advantages and began completing those assignments that were modified using the strategy. With guidance from the school psychologist, Adam's teacher then extended modifications to include pretesting and compacting opportunities across the curriculum. Adam used his time earned from compacting to pursue independent projects and recreational reading, and his behavior problems decreased accordingly.

Conclusion

The focus of educational services for high-ability students is shifting to the regular classroom. While this expansion of services to the regular classroom is a welcome recognition of the need to challenge high-ability students all day, every day, this initiative also brings with it a significant need to train regular education teachers. Support staff such as educators of gifted and talented students and school psychologists must learn to become effective consultants to assist regular classroom teachers in applying instructional strategies appropriate for meeting the needs of high-ability students.

References

Roets, L. (1993). *Modifying standard curriculum for high ability students*. New Sharon, IA: Leadership Publishers.

Winebrenner, S. (1992). *Teaching gifted kids in the regular classroom*. Minneapolis, MN: Free Spirit.

section two

Teaching Strategies

chapter 3

Simulations
active learning for gifted students

by **Danna Garrison May**

he disgruntled chief of police is talking on the telephone while a group of protesters is yelling on the front lawn of City Hall. They all appear to be upset that the city's mayor cut the police force instead of increasing taxes (Wright & Haslam, 1993). Was the right decision made to cut the police force? Should taxes have been raised despite protests? What should the mayor do? It just so happens that you know the mayor very well. In fact, the mayor is one of your students. There is no need to worry, however. Your student is indeed the mayor of this city with some tough decisions to make, but this situation is only a representation of a real situation. This situation is a simulation.

Simulations have been used for centuries. They can be traced back to India more than 1,500 years ago, where the ancient game of chess was first played. Chess was created as a simulation game that dealt with a battle between two nations. Later, a Prussian modified the game, changing the original pieces into representations of actual military units and the game board into a map with models of combat areas. In recent years, this military chess game has been modified for computer war games used in training military personnel.

Researchers have found that simulations are effective in anticipating and preventing possible future international crises and are aids in policy planning in such varied fields as health care and transportation (Lee, 1994).

Positive Effects of Simulations

As a result of the positive and beneficial effects of simulations, their use in the classroom has become popular. Learning must relate to living and surviving in the real world. In simulations, students learn the risks, rewards, costs, and benefits of alternative decision-making strategies (Boocock & Schild, 1968). When implemented effectively, simulations provide an authentic, yet controlled learning experience.

Learning occurs when active experimentation is combined with reflection (Thatcher, 1990). Since all simulations are a form of experiential learning, the involved students will reflect upon the simulation differently. This reflection or debriefing is the key to making the learning experience real, and it often occurs several times during and after the simulation. Topics during debriefing sessions include identifying the effects of the experience; considering the processes developed in the simulation; clarifying the principles, concepts, and facts that were used in the simulation; identifying the emotions involved among the individuals and the group; and identifying the various participant views.

There are three types of simulations. These types include all-machine simulations, person-machine simulations, and all-person simulations.

All-machine simulations are completely computerized. They do have some learning value, but they do not lend themselves to classroom use. They are helpful to researchers, theoreticians, and experimenters.

Person-machine simulations allow individuals or small groups to interact with a computer program (Dukes & Seinder, 1978). Computer simulations are becoming less expensive and are often good representations of real-world processes and systems. *Person-machine* simulations can also be in the form of simulators, such as driver training in which an individual interacts with a mechanical system while making decisions that will affect the outcome of the situation. Simulators are also widely used for pilot and military training (Sweeters, 1994).

The third type is *all-person* simulations. These simulations define the roles of the participants and include a problem in which the participants make choices in their new roles about themselves, the group, their own future, and the outcome of the situation. This type of simulation is particularly classroom friendly and can be used with students of all ages.

Differences in Methods

The terms *simulation*, *role-play*, and *simulation game* are often used interchangeably, but differences do exist. Role-playing is often regarded as performing like another person such as a literary or historical character or a celebrity. Various types of simulations may or may not include role-playing as a component. Simulation games, on the other hand, have a predetermined set of criteria that rewards those who complete the simulation first or who complete the simulation with the highest overall achievement. In simulations, there is no winner (Dukes & Seinder, 1978).

Educators frequently use simulations in the classroom to prepare the student to assume a role in society. Students learn about the elements that affect life and the reasons for outcomes of certain events. For example, in the simulation Choices 2 (Nash & Nash, 1996), students develop possible solutions to real-life problems by writing and acting out minidramas.

Components of a Simulation

Simulations have several basic components. First, the leader presents the problem, which is often something glamorous or exotic such as translating a hieroglyphic message left by a pharaoh 3,000 years ago in Mummy's Message (Maggio, 1996).

Next, the instructor gives the students the information they need to get started, and then the students meet and decide upon their roles in the situation. Each participant develops a role that might require research and planning. From there, the students tackle the situation and eventually present a solution. They check their solution against reality, and they then examine the next problem. The simulation "often culminates in an action-packed finale" (Marks, 1992, p. 26), such as putting Louis XVI and Robespierre on trial in Liberte (Brasefield, 1996) or gathering lords and ladies in a castle for a medieval banquet in Christendom (Hayes, Henderson, & Lacey, 1996).

Advantages of simulations include the use of critical and creative thinking skills such as predicting outcomes, analyzing alternative strategies, and making decisions in a safe, nonthreatening environment, as well as library and scientific research skills, written and verbal communication skills, and leadership skills. Simulations motivate students by using self-discovery. They gain empathy for real-life decisions and a better understanding of the effects of various situations (Lee, 1994). Evidence has shown that simulations increase students' tolerance and their level of acceptance of others' thoughts and ideas (Dukes & Seinder, 1978). Throughout the simulation, students are able to work at different levels that match their experience and abilities.

Despite these obvious advantages, disadvantages exist that relate to time, money, and experience. Simulations demand time to implement effectively, lasting from several hours to several weeks (Marks, 1992). The in-depth learning activities associated with simulations may be delayed or interrupted because of time constraints. Because of the great amount of time that might be involved, the teacher must establish the worth of the simulation so that time may be used effectively. While low-cost simulations have become more readily available over the years, hidden costs exist. To implement some simulations, the school or teacher must purchase extra materials (Taylor & Walford, 1978).

Since simulations may vary depending on the participants' responses, they are difficult to preview (Zuckerman & Horn, 1973). For this reason, first-time users may have different experiences when initially introducing the simulation activity. Everyone involved with the simulation must be patient and attentive while the teacher makes adjustments. Simulations also require an openness and an unquestioning obedience to an arbitrary set of rules and regulations. Since simulations create their own reality, or reconstructs, participants must carefully attend to their personal perceptions of roles within the group such as gender, age, ethnicity, and popularity. The leader or teacher must carefully observe and debrief any kind of stereotyping (McAleese, 1978). Some call these reconstructs "the hidden curriculum of simulations." The hidden curriculum emphasizes technique, strategy, problem solving, and manipulation. Educators who are not familiar with these learning activities often view them as highly complex, difficult to implement, difficult to maintain, and requiring mounds of preparation and paperwork. First-time users may want to begin with a low-maintenance, simple simulation.

While simulations have both advantages and disadvantages, their use is highly recommended with gifted students. Gifted students often enjoy simulations because they allow them to control their own destiny. Students are free to express themselves creatively and make their own decisions, whether right or wrong (Marks, 1992). Simulations motivate gifted students and their teachers to take a more active role in learning and use higher level thinking skills such as researching, discussing, and decision making.

The Teacher's Role

The role of the teacher during simulation activities may be quite different from his or her traditional role in the classroom. The teacher becomes a facilitator, organizer, and manager. To make the simulation run smoothly, teachers may first want to use it with a group of friends or colleagues so that changes can be made before using it in the classroom (Jones, 1987). As the organizer of the activity, the teacher must carefully observe and assess the needs, feelings, and frustrations of the participants during the simulation. The teacher should be detached from the activity, observing from a nonbiased point of view. As the facilitator, "the teacher must have the courage to let the simulation flow" (Thatcher, 1990, p. 271), allowing the students to move through it at the rate and order they choose.

Depending upon the chosen simulation, teachers may want to assign roles, allow students to choose roles, or perhaps have students interview for them. Teachers need to consider group dynamics, as well, before assigning groups or allowing students to choose a particular group (Jones, 1987). During each step of the activity, the teacher assesses the roles of the students and makes sure each is completing his or her fair share of the work. The teacher provides the resources needed for the simulation's success, such as a wide range of research materials and a comfortable environment. Being well acquainted with the subject matter or being willing to admit ignorance, letting go of total control or being able to tolerate chaos, and having the confidence to know that everything will probably work out in the end are essential characteristics of the teacher (Marks, 1990). If the teacher remains flexible and open to adjustments and new ideas, the simulation will work.

Choosing a Model

Besides managing and facilitating simulations, the teacher must choose a debriefing model for the final critical learning and evaluation stage of the simulation. "Until the teacher gives students the opportunity to reflect on their experiences" (Chiodo & Flaim, 1993, p. 119), total learning cannot take place. The student realizes that the simulation is a learning activity, not just a game, during the debriefing process.

Debriefing models may take a variety of forms, such as checklists, informal discussions, structured discussions, or written commentaries (Thatcher, 1990). One such model, called the EIAG model, asks the student to experience, identify, analyze, and generalize the results and procedures used in the simulation. Another model, called the D-FITGA model, asks the students to decompress after the simulation, review related facts associated with the activity, infer and transfer questions and causes that were brought up during the simulation, and generalize and then apply their generalizations to the real world. Either of these models, a combination of the two, and others have all proven to be effective in the debriefing segment. Note that simply summarizing and assessing are not the same as debriefing. The teacher must establish a personal link to the information during debriefing so that the students may become a part of the learning process.

The teacher should use nonthreatening types of assessment that cover a variety of aspects of the simulation. The teacher may assess the students' factual knowledge through more traditional assessment methods such as paper-and-pencil tests and the more complex thinking processes through nontraditional methods. For example, oral and written communication skills, which are often a result of simulation usage, can be assessed through interviews and checklists.

Deciding on a Simulation

Teachers might want to keep several things in mind when choosing simulations. Quality, not quantity, is often the better bargain. The simulation's objectives should match the interests and required ability levels of the students. Teachers need to check to see if the publisher has given permission for documents to be photocopied to avoid the expense of having to order new materials every year. Teachers also need to be aware of the number of participants required by the simulation, the needed implementation materials and space, an approximate time frame for implementation, and the inclusion of a debriefing model.

After using published simulations, teachers and students might decide to design their own, which can be an outstanding learning tool. They need to identify an interesting problem, the roles of the participants, possible solutions, and participant resources. Workable simulations are consistent, plausible, and provide for interaction (Jones, 1987). Thatcher and Robinson's (1990) model for designing simulations is an excellent resource that defines and logically orders the steps for creating an effective simulation.

Conclusion

Using simulations in the classroom can be a challenging, but rewarding experience. Simulations require commitment and energy to merge advanced content and process skills with student interests. Simulations are an excellent form of experiential learning, fostering decision-making and cooperative learning skills. Because of the qualitatively differentiated learning experience they provide, simulations are strongly recommended for use with gifted students.

References

Boocock, S., & Schild, E. (1968). *Simulation games in learning.* Beverly Hills, CA: Sage.

Brasefield, M. (1996). *Liberte: A simulation of the French revolution.* El Cajon, CA: Interact.

Chiodo, J., & Flaim, M. (1993). The link between computer simulations and social studies learning: Debriefing. *Social Studies, 84,* 119–121.

Dukes, R., & Seinder, C. (1978). *Learning with simulations and games.* Beverly Hills, CA: Sage.

Hayes, W., Henderson, M., & Lacey, B. (1996). *Christendom.* El Cajon, CA: Interact.

Jones, K. (1987). *Simulations: A handbook for teachers and training.* New York: Nichols.

Lee, J. (1994). *Effectiveness of the use of simulations in a social studies classroom.* (ERIC Document Reproduction Service No. ED 381448)

Maggio, T. (1996). *Mummy's message.* El Cajon, CA: Interact.

Marks, D. (1992). Training teachers of the gifted to use simulations. *Gifted Child Today, 15*(6), 25–27.

McAleese, R. (1978). *Perspectives on academic gaming and simulation, 3.* New York: Nichols.

Nash, M., & Nash, J. (1996). *Choices 2.* El Cajon, CA: Interact.

Sweeters, W. (1994). Multimedia electronic tools for learning. *Educational Technology, 34*(5), 47–52.

Taylor, J., & Walford, R. (1978). *Learning and the simulation game.* Beverly Hills, CA: Sage.

Thatcher, D. (1990). Promoting learning through games and simulations. *Simulation and Gaming, 21,* 262–273.

Thatcher, D., & Robinson, M. (1990). A simulation on the design of simulations. *Simulation and Gaming, 21,* 256–261.

Wright, W., & Haslam, F. (1993). *Sim City 2000* [Computer software]. Orinda, CA: Maxis.

Zuckerman, D., & Horn, R. (1973). *The guide to simulations/games for education and training.* Lexington, MS: Information Resources.

Simulation Resources

Companies and Publishers

Interact
W5527 State Road 106
P.O. Box 900
Fort Atkinson, WI 53538-0900
(800) 359-0961
http://www.interact-simulations.com

Maxis
2 Theatre Square
Orinda, CA 94563-3346
(510) 254-9700
http://www.maxis.com

Broderbund Software
100 Pine St., Ste. 1900
San Francisco, CA 94111
http://www.broderbund.com

Samples of Published Simulations Categorized by Subject Area

Science

Adapt
Students in grades 6–9 explore a newly discovered continent and decide the best location for a permanent society. Published by Interact.

Earth Friendly
Students in grades 4–10 participate in small groups to create an ecologically sound city that provides safe dwelling for all wildlife and plant life, pollution-free air, and freedom from the threats of toxic waste and nuclear disaster. Published by Prufrock Press.

Endangered Species
Students in grades 4–10 learn about fragile ecologies, discover the impact humans have on nature, solve ecological problems, and develop a deeper appreciation of their ecological responsibilies. Published by Prufrock Press.

Project Polaris
Using estimating and measuring, students in grades 2–6 build a space station. Published by Interact.

Zoo
Students in grades 2–5 have a chance to run a local zoo. Published by Interact.

Language Arts

Enchanted Castle
Students in grades K–4 journey through the fantasy world of fairy tales. Published by Interact.

Library Detective
Using their library research skills, students in grades 4–8 solve a mystery in the library. Published by Interact.

Odyssey
Students in grades 4–8 travel through Greek mythology. Published by Interact.

Social Studies

American Nostalgia
Through a simulated communications corporation, students in grades 7–12 develop and communicate their own ideas about the history and literature of the early 20th century. Published by Prufrock Press.

Calhoun vs. Garrison
Students in grades 7–12 research and debate the issue of slavery in the United States in the mid-1800s. Published by Interact.

Medieval Destinations
Students in grades 9–12 take a simulated flight across England in the Middle Ages, accumulating mileage by studying the history and literature of the period. Published by Prufrock Press.

Pacific Rim
Students in grades 5–9 address the importance of countries who border the Western Pacific Ocean. Published by Interact.

Sim City 4
This simulation is for children of all ages who want to create and run a city. Published by Maxis.

Western Exploration
Students in grades 4–10 journey through the Old West playing the parts of historical characters while exploring the literature, history, culture, and art of the period. Published by Prufrock Press.

Where in the World is Carmen Sandiego?
Carmen Sandiego's Great Chase Through Time
Where in the U.S.A. is Carmen Sandiego?
Students in grades 5–12 learn geographic and historical facts and skills while tracking Carmen across the globe and through time. Published by Broderbund.

Math

Math Quest
Students in grades 3–8 use math problem-solving skills to travel through a magical land. Published by Interact.

Shopping Spree
Using calculator estimation skills, students in grades 3–8 solve problems in given situations. Published by Interact.

Stock Market
Students in grades 6–12 may buy and sell stock. Published by Interact.

chapter 4

How to Use Thinking Skills to Differentiate Curricula for Gifted and Highly Creative Students

by **Andrew Johnson**

ow do we meet the special learning needs of our highly creative and gifted students? Weekly pull-out sessions are often seen as the most common programming option; however, in terms of faculty resources and the overall educational impact on students, this option is the least efficient and effective. Finding ways to differentiate the regular classroom curriculum provides more direct programming and is very economical in terms of additional resources. Tomlinson (1999) suggests that the content, process, and product of a curriculum may be modified. The *content* is the information, concepts, or skills students are to learn. The *process* is the activity students use to manipulate the content or practice the skills. The *product* is the way students demonstrate their knowing. Tomlinson outlines several strategies that a classroom teacher might use to differentiate a curriculum, including stations, agendas, complex instruction, orbital studies, centers, entry points, tiered activities, and learning contracts. A strategy not suggested by Tomlinson, but one that might also be included in this list, is the integration of thinking skills into the curriculum. This article will (a) define thinking skills, (b) describe three common approaches used to teach them, and (c) demonstrate how they can be embedded in any curriculum at all levels.

Defining Thinking Skills

A thinking skill is any cognitive process broken down into a set of explicit steps that are then used to guide thinking (Johnson, 2000b; Perkins, 1986). For example, making inferences or inferring is a cognitive process that is included in many curriculum standards. Inferring is a thinking process that helps one integrate observed clues with background knowledge in order to make an informed guess or prediction. In teaching students to make inferences, the process is broken into these steps: (a) identify the question or point of inference, (b) identify what is known or observed, (c) identify related knowledge that is relevant, and (d) make a reasoned guess based on (b) and (c).

High-Level Thinking

High-level thinking is not the same as a thinking skill. High-level thinking is any cognitive operation that places significant demands on the processing taking place in short term memory, such as analysis, synthesis, and evaluation. Teachers often present high-level thinking tasks without any instruction. All students, including those who are highly creative and intellectually gifted, benefit from being given explicit instruction before being asked to engage in high-level thinking tasks. This instruction helps them learn these cognitive operations more quickly and opens up space in short-term memory that can then be applied to other things.

For example, if the teacher asked students to compare and contrast the character of Lyra in *The Gold Compass* (Pullman, 1995) to Harry Potter in *Harry Potter and the Sorcerer's Stone* (Rowling, 1997), they would be engaged in high-level thinking. But to teach it as a skill, the instructor must break this cognitive process into these steps: (a) look at the whole, (b) find the similarities, (c) find the differences, and (d) describe. The cognitive operation is taught using explicit instruction. With instruction, high-level thinking becomes easier. This idea is the major premise of thinking-skills instruction. Complicated things are made easy by breaking them into parts and teaching them explicitly.

Complex Thinking

Complex thinking is a matter of engaging in cognitive processes that involve many steps or parts. The difference between high-level thinking and complex thinking sometimes is slight. The best example of complex thinking is the thinking process that takes place when planning a lesson for a primary-grade classroom. In planning a lesson, a teacher must (a) define the information or skill to be taught, (b) organize the knowledge or break the skill into manageable parts, (c) decide how to convey this knowledge or teach the skill to students at a level they can understand and in a manner that will keep them focused, (d) create active involvement (e) consider a variety of learning modes, (f) attend to individual differences, (g) manage student behaviors, and (h) design an activity to reinforce the skill or concept. These processes may vary with the teacher and the situation.

In my undergraduate methods course, students often struggle when they are first asked to design lessons. Indeed, it is not reasonable to expect them to know how to engage in the kinds of complex thinking needed to adequately design learning experiences without first providing them explicit instruction. Thus, I break the designing of lesson plans into a few simple, well-defined steps that are taught explicitly (Johnson, 2000a). In planning a lesson, undergraduate students are asked to define their purpose (objective), describe in list or outline form the knowledge or skills needed to support the purpose (input), then design an activity to reinforce the skill or manipulate ideas found in the input (activity). By breaking the complex thinking of lesson design into explicit steps, it becomes a thinking skill that students will be able to master.

Critical and Creative Thinking

Critical thinking is a type of thinking that converges on a single thought or entity. One must organize, analyze, or evaluate information, which might also be broken into parts and taught explicitly. It is only by teaching thinking skills that teachers help students to become better critical thinkers. A cognitive process, complimentary to, but different than critical thinking, is creative thinking. This thinking diverges from a single thought or entity. One must generate, synthesize, find alternatives, adapt, substitute, or elaborate. Each of these operations could also become thinking skills if they were broken into parts and taught explicitly.

Thinking Skills and Thinking Frames

Examples of critical and creative thinking skills and their corresponding thinking frames can be seen in Table 4.1. A thinking frame is a concrete representation of a particular cognitive process broken down into specific steps and used to support the thought process (Johnson, 2000b; Perkins, 1986). These are used to initially guide students' thinking as they learn a thinking skill. Thinking frames can be effectively constructed in poster form and placed in the classroom for teaching and easy review.

Approaches to Thinking Skills Instruction

There are three approaches used in teaching thinking skills: the stand-alone approach, the immersion approach, and the embedded approach (Prawat, 1991).

The Stand-Alone Approach

The stand-alone approach consists of teaching thinking skills separately from subject matter content. In this case, a general set of thinking skills is identified and taught as a separate course or subject. Students are instructed how to transfer the

Table 4.1. **Thinking Frames**

Critical Thinking Skills	Creative Thinking Skills
1. *Inferring:* The student will go beyond the available information to identify what may reasonably be true. *Thinking Frame* A. Identify what is known. B. Identify similar situations. C. Make a reasonable guess based on A and B.	1. *Generate Relationships:* The student will find related items or events. *Thinking Frame* A. Look at the item or event. B. Generate attributes. C. Find items or events with similar or related attributes. D. Describe the relationship.
2. *Compare and Contrast:* Given two or more items, the student will find their similarities and differences. *Thinking Frame* A. Look at all items. B. Find the similarities. C. Find the differences. D. Conclude and describe.	2. *Web and Brainstorm:* The student will create a web to generate ideas relative to a given topic. *Thinking Frame* A. Look at the original ideas. B. Find 2–5 subideas. C. Brainstorm on each subheading. D. Describe.
3. *Creating Groups:* Students will impose order on a field by identifying and grouping common themes or patterns. *Thinking Frame* A. Look at the whole. B. Identify reoccurring items, themes, or patterns. C. Arrange into groups. D. Describe the whole in terms of groups.	3. *Integrate.* The student will connect or combine two or more things to form a new whole. *Thinking Frame* A. Look at both wholes. B. Select interesting or important parts. C. Combine to describe a new whole.

skills to various subjects and situations. The problem with this approach is that students do not have a context in which to learn and use acquired skills. The skills are viewed as puzzles with little relevance to academic or real life tasks. Thinking skills learned in isolation do not transfer well to academic or real world situations (Perkins & Salomon, 1989).

If a classroom teacher were to use this approach to the teaching of thinking skills, students would spend a great deal of time looking at a series of puzzles, word problems, or exercises presented in a workbook. It would be assumed that students would be able to transfer these skills to other situations. However, this transfer would happen in only a few instances.

The Immersion Approach

The immersion approach does not involve teaching thinking skills; rather, it allows good thinking to develop naturally as a result of students being fully engaged or immersed in content-related activities, which call for high levels of thinking. Here, students are provided with repeated practice in complex cognitive activities with the assumption that they will eventually develop the necessary cognitive skills to successfully engage in high-level thinking. As stated previously, simply immersing students in high-level thinking activities is not an effective teaching and learning technique. A series of challenging questions and activities is not a thinking-skills program. If a classroom teacher were to use this approach to the teaching of thinking skills, students would be assigned complex tasks. It would be assumed here that over time, they would be able to discover the steps necessary to complete these complex tasks and develop the appropriate thinking skills. Again, this is not very efficient or effective.

The Embedded Approach

The embedded approach is where thinking skills are taught within a subject matter context. Here, thinking skills are taught in science, social studies, language arts, reading, or some other subject area. Students then apply these skills directly to the particular subject matter being studied. This allows students to use the skills in a meaningful context and helps them learn the subject matter more deeply. An embedded approach is the most effective way to teach thinking skills. Rather than an additional subject, thinking skills are used here to enhance whatever curriculum is currently being taught.

Thinking Skills Embedded Into a Social Studies Unit

Fran Schwartz, a fifth-grade teacher in a cluster classroom, was teaching a social studies unit using newspapers and current events. She wanted assignments or activities that could be used for the intellectually gifted and highly creative students in her room. Below are examples that illustrate how she used thinking skills to create activities for this unit. These activities, which are open-ended and call for high-level thinking, were substituted for the gifted students' regular assignments.

1. *Elaboration.* These are two ways that this thinking skill might be used with newspapers. First, students find a product in an ad and look for ways to improve the product or the ad. Or, the teacher pulls sentences or paragraphs from the newspaper and students find ways to make them more interesting.

2. *Flexibility.* Using a sentence or paragraph in the newspaper, students generate as many ways to express the same idea as they can.

3. *Originality.* Students find a product from a newspaper ad and design their own video commercials, signs, or newspaper ads.

4. *Integrate.* Using newspaper ads for different products, students combine them to come up with a brand-new product or device. Then, they create a newspaper ad for their new product.

5. *Creating Groups.* Students record newspaper headlines over a period of time and put them into groups. The types of groups and frequency of items in each group are reported. These data

can be graphed and comparison can be made with other newspapers, types of publications, or time periods.

6. *Compare and Contrast.* Students compare a 200-word section of a headline story to a 200-word section of a sports story. What is similar? Different? This can be extended by comparing and contrasting a newspaper section with a section from a textbook and a narrative book or by comparing one newspaper to another.

7. *Analysis.* Students examine the newspaper to determine one or all of the following: What goes into a newspaper? What makes up a sports section? What comprises a news section, want ads, entertainment section, and so on? Who makes these decisions? Why do some newspapers include some sections and others do not?

8. *Investigation.* Students examine a 100-word section of newspaper text. An inquiry is designed by asking one ore more of the following questions: What are the parts of this section? How many sentences? Adjectives? How many adjectives per sentence? What is the average length of each sentence? These data can be graphed and comparisons can be made to other types of text.

9. *Inference.* Students select an editorial and use the Infer-O-Gram to make inferences about the author (see Figure 4.1). The inference question might be how might we describe the writer of this editorial? Who is this author? What kind of person is this author? What political party does this author belong to? Students list clues from the editorial on the left side, and clues from what they know on the right.

10. *Creative Problem Solving.* Students identify a problem found in the newspaper (i.e., problems might also be taken from the school, community, or classroom). In small groups, students generate solutions, pick the best solution, refine and embellish it, then present their solutions to the class. Examples of problems: How can we reduce crime in our neighborhood? How can we prevent teenage smoking? How

Question: _____

Clues from the text	Clues that I know

Figure 4.1. **Infer-o-gram**

can we make the lunch line go faster? How can we solve the fighting that is happening on the playground? How can we come to a consensus on an issue?

11. *Evaluation/Critique.* Students define the criteria for a good movie. This naturally leads to discussions about movie genre. Then newspaper ads are found for movies students have seen. Students rate these movies on their criteria (see Figure 4.2).

Thinking Skills and Tiered Assignments

Thinking skills can also be used to create tiered assignments, one of the classroom differentiation strategies described by

Movie title: _____

Criteria	Rating
Has a good plot or story.	
Has plenty of action.	
Has interesting lead characters.	
Has good special effects.	

Rating: 4 = very high, 3 = good, 2 = average, 1 = low

Figure 4.2. Rating movies

Tomlinson (1999). A *tiered assignment* or activity is where students manipulate or practice the same concept or skill; however, they do so at differing levels of complexity and sophistication. For example, after reading a chapter on dinosaurs, the following five activities could be used to manipulate the same concepts: (a) name the five meat-eating dinosaurs described in the chapter, (b) use the web and brainstorm strategy to describe three interesting or important ideas about meat-eating dinosaurs, (c) compare and contrast a meat-eating dinosaur and an elephant, (d) put the meat-eating dinosaurs into groups, or (e) support the statement, the Tyrannosaurus Rex was a meat-eating dinosaur.

To create a tiered assignment, a teacher first identifies pivotal concepts or understanding that all students should learn. Then, two or three activities are created of varying levels of difficulty or complexity. Although five activities are described above, use no more than two or three levels or tiers for each assignment. Some teachers like to assign students to specific tiers. Others like to provide options and let students select which assignment tier they prefer. Even though both options can be used, the latter may be more preferred for two reasons:

First, all students enjoy choice and the empowerment that comes with it. Second, students will naturally gravitate to the level that is best suited to them. In this way, teachers find students who display high levels of thinking that were previously not noticed.

The Final Word

Embedding thinking skills into a lesson or curriculum is a fairly simple and cost effective way to begin the process of differentiated instruction for gifted and highly creative students. It works particularly well for creating tiered assignments in a clustered classroom. However, thinking skills can also be used to enhance the curriculum for all students.

References

Johnson, A. (2000a). It's time for Madeline Hunter to go. *Action in Teacher Education, 22*, 72–78.

Johnson, A. (2000b). *Up and out: Using creative and critical thinking skills to enhance learning.* Needham Heights, MA: Allyn and Bacon.

Perkins, D. N. (1986). Thinking frames. *Educational Leadership, 42*, 4–10.

Perkins, D. N., & Salomon, G. (1989). Are cognitive skills context bound? *Educational Researcher, 47*, 16–25.

Prawat, R. (1991). Embedded thinking skill instruction in subject matter instruction. In A. Costa (Ed.), *Developing minds* (Vol. 1, pp. 185–186). Alexandria, VA: Association for Supervision and Curriculum Development.

Pullman, P. (1995). *The gold compass.* New York: Del Rey.

Rowling, J. K. (1997). *Harry Potter and the sorcerer's stone.* New York: Scholastic Press.

Tomlinson, C. A. (1999). *The differentiated classroom: Responding to the needs of all learners.* Alexandria, VA: Association for Supervision and Curriculum Development.

chapter 5

Developing a Foundation for Independent Study

by **Steffi Pugh**

Student design and implementation of independent study contracts is an important developmental piece of the ninth-grade curriculum of the Downingtown Educational Enrichment Program (DEEP). This program serves identified gifted students at the Downingtown High Ninth Grade Center through a yearlong scheduled elective course option that meets every other day and offers one-half credit.

The intent of the independent study contract portion of the program is to build upon individual student interest while encouraging development and application of key skills in higher order thinking and problem solving. While the teacher provides a general framework for contract organization, each student must develop components of topic selection, inquiry questioning, predicting, planning, scheduling, investigating, problem solving, creating, and self-evaluation. To prepare students for this challenging project and to facilitate understanding of the underlying strategies needed, all students participate in a thinking skills foundation program during the first marking period of the school year.

Critical Thinking Skills Foundation Program: Overview and Design

Critical thinking skills are addressed through a 2-week unit entitled "Bloom's Taxonomy: Critical Thinking in Action." Students investigate Bloom's Taxonomy of the Cognitive Domain (Bloom, 1956) through a combination of group and individual activities. Group projects reinforce understanding and application of Bloom's taxonomy through the upgrading of end-of-chapter textbook questions, the composing of varied level questions, and the identification and classification of the levels of teacher-prepared questions. Each student then develops a final independent study project based on a topic of individual interest with guiding questions representing all six levels of Bloom's taxonomy. When carried over to the development of the independent study contract, this process enables students to ask critical questions that will drive independent higher order investigation of self-selected topics.

Rationale: Positive Effects of Higher Level Student Questioning

The ability to generate increasingly complex questions is an integral part of student investment in the learning process. There is a direct correlation between self-directed inquiry and increased motivation and persistence in gifted student learners (deCharms, 1976; Deci, 1985; Hayes-Jacobs & Borland, 1986; Stipek & Weisz, 1981). In addition, student design of higher level questioning fosters the synthesis of concepts and leads to well-developed responses. By asking their own provocative questions, students learn how to approach problems comprehensively and elicit their own in-depth answers. The empowering nature and positive outcome of student-generated higher level questioning make it a powerful tool for fully engaging ninth-grade gifted students in challenging self-selected study.

Implementing Bloom's Taxonomy: Critical Thinking in Action

The 2-week critical thinking foundation program is set up to review previously taught concepts, preassess current levels of understanding, and then spend the remainder of the time reinforcing and enhancing understanding through multiple applications and opportunities for interactive and independent lesson format. Students receive a unit guide sheet that summarizes the daily activity sequence and instructions, as well as a packet containing all reference materials. The sequence and content of instruction are as follows:

1. *Review of Bloom's taxonomy, levels, and value verbs.*
   The introductory class period is spent on a condensed review of the theoretical base, levels, and value verbs of Bloom's taxonomy. Sample questions for each level are modeled and students are asked to contribute further examples orally.

2. *Identification of taxonomic levels (preassessment).*
   During the following class period, a preassessment is administered that measures student ability to identify the taxonomic level of given questions or commands (see Figure 5.1).

3. *Writing questions on each level.*
   On the third day, students begin to devise their own questions at varied levels of Bloom's taxonomy. The students are encouraged to use reference lists of the taxonomy's value verbs to help them individually write three questions at each level. All work is shared with the class group.

4. *Raising the level of questions.*
   The fourth day's activity requires students to both identify and raise the level of textbook questions. After the students have each chosen a school textbook, they each turn to the review questions at the end of one chapter and identify the taxonomic levels of the questions. Next, they rewrite the questions to raise the level of thinking and identify the new taxonomic level of each question. The students then share

The questions/commands below address the following paradox: "America is a great and rich country, yet a great amount of poverty exists."

Identify the level of each question or command and write the corresponding initial for that level in each blank: K = Knowledge, C = Comprehension, AP = Application, AN = Analysis, S = Synthesis, E = Evaluation. Review your answers with the teacher as a group and then submit work to the teacher.

_____ Summarize the characteristics of an economically deprived community.

_____ Design an economic system that would eliminate poverty.

_____ How many families live with an income below the average?

_____ Given three utopia societies, if you were poor, which one should you prefer to live under and why?

_____ List the causes of poverty. Why do poor communities develop?

_____ How could some of these approaches be used to solve the problem of poverty here in St. Paul?

_____ Construct a chart showing the various economic levels of the various areas of Downingtown.

_____ Which states have the greatest poverty problems?

_____ Think of the problems that would arise if there were no poverty in the U.S.

_____ Compare these problems with the problems that poverty causes. Rate both sides.

_____ Tell what percent of Americans are classified as disadvantaged.

_____ In your own words, tell what it would be like to be poor and live in a depressed area.

_____ If your family were poor, what would or could you do?

_____ What would happen if all men were to share the total wealth of the nation?

_____ Describe the kind of communities that are in poverty.

_____ Specify the conditions of a person that might cause him or her to be poor.

_____ Come up with four forms of government that would eliminate the poverty problem. List criteria that would be necessary for rating the effectiveness of these forms.

_____ Specify the conditions under which a free enterprise system might lead to poverty.

_____ Compare and contrast Exton to the Chester Springs area.

_____ Consider one condition leading to poverty and create a solution to this problem.

Figure 5.1. Identification of taxonomic levels

Raising the Level of Questions

Assignment: Using one of your school textbooks, turn to the review questions at the end of one chapter. Identify levels of the questions. Then, rewrite the questions to raise the level of thinking. Share with the group and submit work to the teacher.

Examples: (From the textbook *Exploring World Culture*)

p. 545:
Old question: Describe early migration to the Americas.
    Taxonomic level: **Comprehension**

New question: Draw a map of early migration to the Americas.
    Taxonomic level: **Application**

p. 549:
Old question: Describe methods the Spaniards used to control the empire.
    Taxonomic level: **Comprehension**

New question: Invent ways Spaniards could have used to control their empire.
    Taxonomic level: **Synthesis**

p. 557:
Old Question: What benefits did the coming of the Spanish bring to the native peoples of the Americas?
    Taxonomic level: **Knowledge / Comprehension**

New question: Rank and evaluate the benefits the Spanish brought to the native peoples of the Americas.
    Taxonomic level: **Evaluation**

Figure 5.2. **Sample activity**

all questions (original and revised) with the class group (see Figure 5.2).

5. *Final Bloom's taxonomy project and postassessment.*
    After finishing all prior group and individual work on the Bloom's taxonomy unit, each student completes a 2-week independent project as a culminating activity. The project can be of a student's own creative design, but it must

reflect mastery of Bloom's conceptual levels. Each student selects a topic of personal interest and develops six questions or commands pertaining to the topic, one at each successive level of Bloom's taxonomy. Students are reminded to elaborate in all responses and to cite criteria to support evaluations. It is explained that many of their answers will be in written format, while other responses (depending on the choice of question or command verb) may be interpreted orally, visually, musically, or kinesthetically. An idea menu is provided for diverse products (Campbell, Campbell, & Dickinson, 1996). Students discuss proposals for their final projects with the teacher and are given copies of the evaluation rubric to review (see Figure 5.3 and 5.4). Upon completion of the assignment, students fill out the self-evaluation portion of the rubric and turn it in with the project.

Follow-Up: Development of Contracts for Independent Study

Once students have successfully demonstrated their ability to construct and complete an independent project with higher order guiding questions, they are ready to begin developing more complex independent study contracts that will require them to incorporate acquired critical thinking and problem-solving skills with planning and organization skills. To complete the contract and initiate independent study, students must

- select a topic of personal interest;
- pose a problem to investigate or a challenge to solve;
- develop six guiding inquiry questions;
- develop a step-by-step plan for implementing the project and answering all questions;
- establish a timeline for completing each step of the project plan;
- predict possible difficulties or problems that could arise during project work;
- propose solution(s) to those problems;
- select at least three criteria for teacher and self-evaluation;
- self-evaluate based on above criteria (self-evaluation using

teacher-designed independent study rubric is also required); and

- list all reference materials used to complete the project (bibliography).

With examples provided and teacher guidance available, students can generate realistic and workable plans for pursuing independent study (see Figure 5.5).

Most importantly, students can incorporate a higher level questioning component into their contract design that will enhance the level of thinking and improve the overall quality of their work. By completing the thinking skills foundation unit on Bloom's taxonomy prior to beginning independent study, students gain the confidence needed to undertake the complex task of designing their own challenging learning tasks.

Program Evaluation

Evaluation of the "Bloom's Taxonomy: Critical Thinking in Action" skills program was conducted through analysis of student rubric scores. Additional student feedback was received via an oral program critique and review at the end of the school year. Overall, the student performance review at the end of the program indicated that most students demonstrated a high degree of facility in applying strategies of Bloom's taxonomy to the development of increasingly complex questions and responses. Students became quite skilled in generating thought-provoking questions and became correspondingly adept at composing elaborate and in-depth responses. As a group, their level of confidence in undertaking independent study was significantly enhanced and their enthusiasm for producing high-quality work notably increased.

The topics of study were diverse, ranging from investigations of virtual architectural design on computers, to the writing of a science fiction novelette. Some students worked primarily within the framework of the DEEP classroom environment, while others extended projects to include interdisciplinary or extracurricular activities involving additional students, teachers, or outside sources. One student explored the subject of

0: Poor: (does not do required work; disorganized; incomplete; unrealistic; does not contribute to group activity)
1: Below average: (work is carelessly done; not working to ability; minimum elaboration and/or participation)
2: Standard performance: (steps properly followed; adequate elaboration and/or participation)
3: High proficiency: (well-reasoned; well-substantiated; well-supported; active participation)
4: Outstanding performance: (originality shown in all steps; leadership shown in group participation)

54–60 score pts. = **Outstanding (grade A)**; 48–53 score pts.= **Satisfactory+ (grade B)**; 42–47 score pts. = **Satisfactory- (grade C)**; 35–41 score pts. = **Unsatisfactory (grade D)**; 0–35 score pts. = **Unsatisfactory (grade F)**

	Self-Evaluation	Teacher Evaluation
Student contributed constructively to Bloom's group discussion and problem solving	**0 1 2 3 4** Comments:	**0 1 2 3 4** Comments:
Work was completed and handed in on time: 2 = on time 1 = 1 day late (unexcused) 0 = 2 or more days late	**0 1 2** Comments:	**0 1 2** Comments:
Good copy of final project is in ink or typed, legible 2 = inked or typed, double-spaced, highly legible 1 = inked or typed, but single-spaced or less readable 0 = not inked or typed, or difficult to read	**0 1 2** Comments:	**0 1 2** Comments:
Mechanics of final project are correct (spelling, punctuation, capitalization). 2 = generally correct 1 = minor or infrequent errors 0 = numerous or critical errors	**0 1 2** Comments:	**0 1 2** Comments:
Process/Format Score:	_____	_____

Figure 5.3. **Rubric for process/format**

	Self-Evaluation	Teacher Evaluation
Understanding of Bloom's Taxonomy was demonstrated through group work and individual final project.	0 1 2 3 4 Comments:	0 1 2 3 4 Comments:
(Final project): Bloom's steps are illustrated completely, clearly, and correctly. Questions are well-constructed.	0 1 2 3 4 Comments:	0 1 2 3 4 Comments:
(Final project): Answers are detailed, elaborate, clear, and well-organized.	0 1 2 3 4 Comments:	0 1 2 3 4 Comments:
(Final project): Analysis, Synthesis, and Evaluation level responses are adequately developed.	0 1 2 3 4 Comments:	0 1 2 3 4 Comments:
(Final project): Work shows creativity, exhibits fluency.	0 1 2 3 4 Comments:	0 1 2 3 4 Comments:

Content Score: _____ _____

+ Process/Format Score: _____ _____

= Combined Score/Grade: _____ _____

Figure 5.4. **Rubric for content**

Name __Josh R.__ Date __2/10__

I. **General Area of Study** __theater set design and production/direction__

    I.E.P. Goal Area(s) Emphasized__creativity, research, and independence/planning/responsibility__

    M. I. Area(s) Emphasized__visual/spatial (also bodily/kinesthetic and interpersonal)__

II. **Facts Known About General Area—Why This Interest You:**

> I am very interested in all aspects of drama and have participated in numerous school and community theater productions. I have had some experience working on theatrical sets, but I would like to learn more about methods, materials, and designs that can be used. I would also like to try my hand at directing a production crew.

III. **Problem Statement:** State a concise, clear, and specific problem to be studied.

> After researching ways in which theater sets can be made and used and studying the script for Shakespeare's play The Comedy of Errors, I will design a functional and attractive set for the play. I will follow this by directing others in building the set.

IV. **Questions to be Considered:** Include all levels of thinking; label each question.
Question: K   C   Ap   An   S   E

1. What is the location and setting of each opening scene of the play? Describe in detail. (C)
2. Where, when, and how do settings change during each scene in the script? (An)
3. How do various methods of designing and building sets work? Compare and contrast. (An)
4. (For The Comedy of Errors) What type of set would be the most cost-effective to build? The most practical set to use? Which type of set would enhance perfomance most? (E)
5. What original plan can I design for the set that would meet the above criteria? Create a sketch of the plan. (S)
6. What supplies will be needed to build the set? List them. (K)
7. (Together with production crew members) What must be done to build the set? Convert sketches into transparencies, project designs on display boards, paint, etc.) (Ap)

V. **Plan**

    A. Steps to Be Taken: Enumerate logical steps and the order in which they must be accomplished.

1. Review the play script. Answer questions #1 and #2.
2. Research theater set design techniques and materials and take notes. Locate reference books and consult with Mrs. Pugh (DEEP) and Mr. McCloskey (Theater Arts). Answer question #3.
3. Determine the best idea for set design based on low cost, practicality, and enhancement of performance. Answer question #4. Conference with student play directors, Mrs. Pugh, and Mr. McCloskey to review ideas and critique.
4. Sketch/design my original set. Answer question #4.
5. Make a list of all needed supplies to build the set. Determine roles, number of people, and schedule/location needed for production crew meetings. Recruit and organize. Consult teachers for help.

Figure 5.5. **Contract for independent study**

6. *Gather all needed supplies: foam boards, transparencies, projectors, paint, tarps, brushes, etc. Check with Mrs. Pugh, Mr. McCloskey, and the maintenance department.*
7. *Build the set!*

B. Anticipate Difficulties (obstacles, disappointments, etc.) **and Predict How You Will Deal With Them.**

Accessing enough info. might be a challenge. I will ask my teachers and librarian for help. Coming up with a practical way to switch sets during scenes will be tough. I'll have to be creative. Materials could be costly. I might need to use recycled or donated supplies. Arranging a workable production schedule that suits everyone could be difficult. I will try to be flexible and work around conflicts. Making sure production members get along and get everything done could be hard. I will have to work out roles and duties ahead of time so we are efficient.

C. Schedule: Draw up a schedule using your starting date and your anticipated completion date to show when each of your major steps will be complete.

Begin project: 2/10
Complete Step 1: 2/17 (approx. 2 class periods)
Complete Step 2: 2/27 (approx. 4 class periods)
Complete Step 3: 3/9   (approx. 3 class periods)
Complete Step 4: 3/17 (approx. 3 class periods)
Complete Step 5: 3/25 (approx. 3 class periods)
Complete Step 6: 4/2   (approx. 1 week/ outside of class)
Complete Step 7: 5/4   (will require production meetings outside of class)

Estimated Completion Date: _5/4 (play performance date: 5/19)_

VI. What will the results of this project be? (See M.I. menu: examples—writing, artwork, drama, music, science experiment, game, etc.) Correspond project format to selected M.I. area.

original theater sets designed for the play A Comedy of Errors (visual/spatial M.I.)

VII. List three criteria upon which you anticipate your project will be able to be fairly evaluated.

• *Effective info. gathering and application of research to set design*
• *Creativity of design*
• *Demonstration of organization, planning, and leadership skills*

VIII. Approval

Teacher signature_ S. Pugh _____   Student signature_ Josh R. _____

IX. Bibliography: Include or attach a bibliography citing sources.

Holt, Michael. _Stage Design and Properties_. Phaedon Press, 1995.
James, Thurston. _The Theater Props Handbook: A Comprehensive Guide to Theater Properties, Materials, and Construction_. Betterway Publications, 1990.
Sweet, Harvey. _Handbook of Scenery, Properties, and Lighting: Scenery and Props_. Prentice Hall, 1994.

X. Self-Evaluation: (attach additional sheet as needed)

I think that I did very well on this project. I was able to gather a lot of recycled materials and to organize a production team that worked together to implement my plans for the set. The reversible set design worked out excellently and we even won an award for "Most Creative Set" at the Shakespeare Festival. Even though I had to put a great deal of effort into this assignment, I had fun working on it most of the time and I learned a lot in the process, too!

glass, creating a photo-journalistic record of her visit to a glass-blowing studio and then designing her own stemware. Several students learned sign language and made a video recording of their signing stories and poems they had written. Josh, a student with high interest and ability in dramatic arts, studied theater set design and led a production crew in the creation of sets for a student performance of Shakespeare's *A Comedy of Errors*. In competition at the annual Shakespeare Festival held at Immaculata College, Josh's design and direction efforts were recognized when the production crew received an award for "Most Creative Set" (see Figure 5.5 for description and documentation of Josh's independent study contract and project).

While the products of each DEEP student's independent study may have differed considerably, the questions that drove their studies were similar in that the levels of challenge were consistent. This commonality set a true standard for performance that was readily accepted and promoted by most of the students. As a precursor to student-designed independent study, the thinking skills foundation program established a baseline for what constituted "acceptable" student work, raising the quality of independent study products immensely.

In addition, the opportunity to apply thinking skills to the development of an organized plan for self-directed study represented an important step in the developmental growth of these adolescent students. They learned quickly that responsibility for and ownership of one's own learning are critical to achieving success in high school and beyond. As Clark (1997) observed, "Success, achievement, and well-being come with personal power and the perception of inner control" (p. 335). Promoting the development of higher level thinking skills truly facilitates an array of positive independent learning skills in secondary gifted students.

References

Bloom, B. (Ed.). (1956). *Taxonomy of educational objectives. Handbook I: Cognitive domain*. New York: McKay.

Campbell, L., Campbell, B., & Dickinson, D. (1996). *Teaching and learning through multiple intelligences*. Needham Heights, MA: Allyn and Bacon.

Clark, B. (1997). *Growing up gifted: Developing the potential of children at home and at school* (5th ed.). Upper Saddle River, NJ: Prentice Hall.

deCharms, R. (1976). *Enhancing motivation: Change in the classroom.* New York: Halsted.

Deci, E. (1985). The well-tempered classroom. *Psychology Today, 19*(3), 52–53.

Hayes-Jacobs, H., & Borland, J. (1986). The interdisciplinary concept model: Theory and practice. *Gifted Child Quarterly, 30,* 159–163.

Stipek, D., & Weisz, J. (1981). Perceived personal control and academic achievement. *Review of Educational Research, 51,* 101–137.

chapter 6

The 2–5–8 Plan
*reaching all children
through differentiated assessment*

by **Laura Magner**

*t*eachers today are called upon more and more to adjust the instruction in the classroom to fit each child's needs and foster his or her talents. As a classroom teacher with a gifted cluster, I have borrowed and developed different strategies to differentiate the curriculum for my students. I use pretesting in order to group my students and to compact the regular curriculum. "Tic–Tac–Toe" assignment boards are also an excellent way to allow for student choice (Winebrenner, 1992).

While choice is important in a classroom community, there are times when the presentation of new curricula may need to be the same for all students. If the content is the same, then the assessment may be differentiated. This can be done through various projects.

A 2–5–8 Assessment Plan can offer much flexibility to the teacher. This plan can be used in any subject area, as well as any grade level. The codes 2, 5, and 8 refer to the codes that the assessment choices are given. The students are given an average of three choices for each code. They may choose any assignments that total to 10. For example, a student may wish to do one code 2 and one code 8; another student may choose to do two code 5s. They *may not* choose to do five code 2s. Because the codes are assigned by difficulty, a teacher does not want a student to do too many simple tasks. However, a student *may* choose one code 5 and one code 8, which totals more than 10, and thereby be eligible for extra credit.

What is a 2–5–8 Assessment Plan?

Based on Bloom's taxonomy, each code pulls from two areas of thinking skills. Code 2 assessment choices center on knowledge and comprehension. These choices ask students to tell, recite, define, and locate. They may complete a quiz or short test, define vocabulary, give facts, and so on.

To follow an elementary unit on geometry, code 2 assessment selections may look as follows:

2   Draw and define five plane and five space figures.
2   Given a page of 10 drawn angles, label each angle as acute, right, or obtuse. Draw two acute, right, and obtuse angles using a ruler or protractor.
2   Looking around the classroom, find and chart everyday objects that have square, rectangle, triangle, and circle faces. Record at least three classroom objects for each shape.

The middle code 5 has assessment choices that fall into the average difficulty range and focus on application and analysis. Choices in this code range reflect the student's ability to use and demonstrate information, classify and categorize, solve problems, and compare and contrast. Examples of code 5 assessments are as follows:

5   Draw a picture of a real-life landscape. Outline and label each right angle black, each set of parallel lines red, and each pair of perpendicular lines blue.
5   Design a plan for a cube, and be able to demonstrate how to fold paper into a cube. How many square faces does a

cube have? Design a plan for a rectangle. How is this plan like or unlike the plan for the cube?

5   Develop and share Venn diagrams that compare and contrast plane shapes to their corresponding space shape (square to cube, rectangle to rectangular prism, triangle to pyramid, and circle to sphere).

The highest code's assessment choices require upper level thinking skills. Students who choose these assessments are asked to evaluate and synthesize. These outcomes may include debates, critiques, informed decisions, stories, advertisements, and inventions. Code 8 examples are as follows:

8   Create a nontraditional living space—a home with no rectangles. Use pyramids, prisms, and/or cylinders. Draw a blueprint of the house. Prepare an advertisement (print, radio, or television) to market this unusual home. Present your advertisement to classmates.

8   Design and build a model of an invention using different sizes of rectangular prisms only. Write a short description about the kind of work your invention makes easier. Explain your invention to the class.

8   Photograph or draw a representational picture of real life objects that illustrate the following geometric terms or concepts. Label each picture with the term and the location of the object. (Terms: polygon, parallel lines, perpendicular lines, congruent, an example of a flip, a slide, a half turn, an acute angle, a right angle, an obtuse angle.) Present your pictures to the class. Describe which geometric principles were the hardest/easiest to find in the real world. Why do you suppose they were difficult/easy?

For the previous geometry assessment example, three choices were given for each code. Teachers may adjust the model as needed. You may choose to offer four choices for code 5, but only three choices for codes 2 and 8.

The 2–5–8 Plan is easy for students to understand. I recommend posting the plan in the classroom during the unit of study. This way, the students will be familiar with the choices. When the time comes, record each individual's chosen assessments on an informal chart or contract. Class time is given for the completion of the assessments, just as it would for a "normal" test. How much time is given, or how many class days depends on the codes and how involved you wish to get. Whatever you decide, record the due date on the contract. For this Geometry 2–5–8, I would allow two days of math time and may give the option to work on the assessments as homework.

The teacher's job during the assessment time is to act as a facilitator and resource. The teacher should rotate around the room assisting, redirecting, and encouraging students as needed. Any materials needed should be readily available.

How Do I Grade These Assessments?

With so many choices, how is it possible to grade these assessments and provide useful feedback to the students? Each code assessment can be scored and entered in a grade book separately, or the code scores can be merged to arrive at one "test" score worth a total of 100%.

In 2–5–8, a base-10 percentage can be assigned to each code. A code 2 assessment is 20% of the grade, a code 5 is 50% of the grade, and a code 8 is 80% of the grade. The only rule students have to follow is that the sum of the codes they pick must equal 10, which in turn will equal 100% (except for those who chose to go beyond for extra credit).

I recommend using a rubric to score the assessments (see Figure 6.1). The information on a rubric is helpful to a student, more so than a solitary number score. On the rubric, for editing, an 8 out of 10 possible on the continuum tells the child that they did not fully edit their submission. The rubric is also a good communicator to the parent. You may use it, alter it, or create one of your own. Be sure that the specific skills that you are assessing are weighted heavily and noted clearly on the rubric. Go over the rubric with the students so they are familiar with each scale and how to achieve full credit for each area. I also suggest posting the rubric in the classroom. The student must know what is being expected before beginning the assessment process.

In the geometry example, the first scale for each code is "*All skills are represented correctly.*" This means the teacher is looking

Name _____ Date completed _____

CODE 2 (if chosen) Assessment description _____

Skills are incorrectly told or omitted.	Some skills are retold.	All skills are represented correctly.
1	5	10

Work is disorganized, sloppy.	Work is relatively neat and partially edited.	Work is completely edited.
1	5	10

Code 2 Total _____ / 20 points

CODE 5 (if chosen) Assessment description _____

Skills are incorrectly told or omitted.	Some skills are retold.	All skills are represented correctly.
1	10	20

Work shows little thought.	Work is original.	Work is original and creative.
1	10	20

Work is disorganized, sloppy.	Work is relatively neat and partially edited.	Work is completely edited.
1	5	10

Code 5 Total _____ / 50 points

CODE 8 (if chosen) Assessment description _____

Skills are incorrectly told or omitted.	Some skills are retold.	All skills are represented correctly.
1	15	30

Work shows little thought.	Work is original.	Work is original, creative, and novel.
1	15	30

Work is disorganized, sloppy.	Work is relatively neat and partially edited.	Work is completely edited.
1	5	10

Class presentation is disorganized, hard to hear.	Presentation was organized, mostly audible.	Project was well presented and easily heard.
1	5	10

Code 8 Total _____ / 80 points

Assessment Total _____ / 100 points

Figure 6.1. **2–5–8 scoring rubric**

for correct use or interpretation of the geometric principles discussed in class, such as parallel lines, perpendicular lines, the difference between plane and space figures, examples of those figures, and so on.

Another way to evaluate the 2–5–8 Assessment Plan is to assign a check, a check minus, or a check minus, minus to each assessment. A check is full credit. Therefore a student would earn the full 20%, 50%, or 80% mentioned above. A check minus is an average effort, and is equal to around an 80%, or C value. Numbers representing 80% would be 16/20, 40/50, and 64/80. A check minus, minus is a failing score. Some work was attempted, but it falls short of grade level expectations. These scores representing 50% are 10/20, 25/50, and 40/80. Scores assigned to a student's work can be added together to arrive at a total score out of 100 points.

Students enjoy the chance to choose their assessment. The 2–5–8 Plan lends itself to the flexibility needed in today's classrooms. Teachers in the regular classroom, as well as gifted resource rooms, can use this model to differentiate assessments in any subject area for all ages. This plan for assessment can allow children to show off and use their talents, as well as branch out and express their knowledge base in new ways.

References

Winebrenner, S. (1992). *Teaching gifted kids in the regular classroom.* Minneapolis, MN: Free Spirit.

chapter 7

Problem Solving
and Gifted Education
a differentiated fantasy unit

by **Kenneth Smith** *and* **Michele Weitz**

*i*magine three types of students in your classroom. One student is a traditional "schoolhouse" gifted student who tests well, picks up new concepts quickly, and displays an overall interest and aptitude for established academics. Another student is a nontraditional gifted student who has an extremely high intellect, but does not perform well in traditional tasks, and who reasons better when allowed to study and perform in a way that fosters a nontraditional style. A third student is one who has particular strengths or interests within an array of personal abilities, but may not be viewed as gifted on recognized measures.

How can a literature unit be designed to provide for the special needs of these three kinds of students? Renzulli's (1998) schoolwide enrichment and Tomlinson's (1995, 1999) differentiated instruction models, combined with research in problem solving (Bereiter, Burtis, & Scardamalia, 1988; McCutchen, 1986; Smith, 1995; Wineburg, 1991), inspired the fifth-grade teachers at Sunset Ridge School in Northfield, IL, to design a unit on fantasy that did just that. The unit had two overlapping segments. First, students worked in small groups exploring a novel to learn the germane content and genre characteristics. Then, students regrouped to refine and apply what they had learned to a variety of open-ended problems—in the process, creating a representation of their knowledge to share with other students. In all parts of the unit, instruction was differentiated to foster individual strengths, creativity, and interests.

In the problem-solving literature, many researchers distinguish between problems where there is one correct answer (e.g., multiplication equations) and those where the solver finds aspects of quality, open-ended solutions (e.g., choreographing a dance). The best solution path to the former, though possibly complex, is evident to experts, whereas there are multiple quality solutions in the latter situation, all of which are laden with options. Many studies indicate that beginners deal with the multifaceted nature of such open-ended problems by ignoring structural (or genre) information and limiting the amount of content that they bring to bear on the solutions (e.g., Chi, Hutchinson, & Robin, 1989; McCutchen, 1986; Smith, 1995.) The unit projects presented in this article are designed to guide all students in the class to integrate more content and genre information into their solutions of open-ended problems in ways that match their learning styles and intellectual levels.

The Fantasy Unit

Initially, all the students in the grade were given a list of books selected by the teaching team for their genre (fantasy) characteristics, literary quality, gender representation, and range of reading levels. The books were listed from easiest to most challenging, and the descriptions not so subtly reflected this gradation (see Appendix A for a list of books used in the unit). Students were asked to rank order their choice of books and eliminate any that they had already read. All of the books were displayed for review, and students were discouraged from making this a strictly "social" decision. Most students seemed to make selections that were appropriate for their reading ability; however, a few chose books that were probably pushing their instructional level. Whether a social decision or a reflection on how interested they were in a particular novel, students were supported in their decisions.

Once in their book groups, students participated in literature circles. These circles were complemented by activities representative of the kinds of problems faced in the second part of the unit. The literature circles were student-led discussions based on the roles and responsibilities as detailed in Harvey Daniels' *Literature Circles: Voice and Choice in the Student-Centered Classroom* (1994).

These circles allowed students to master content and genre aspects of the novels through a formalized discussion process. Each student was assigned a role connected to a different strength or focus: Artful Artist draws the passage at hand; Discussion Director ensures that all members participate and develop questions for the group; Word Finder identifies and defines important words in the passages; and Passage Picker, within a given range of pages, selects the passages for their imagery, relevance, or interest. Roles rotate at each session. If groups are large, more students can share a role, or the group can be divided into smaller groups that compare their results at the end of the session (see Appendix B for a set of sample questions). The literature circle proved especially successful in encouraging all students to ask questions and respond to each other's comments. The variety of roles allowed students with particular strengths to employ them to analyze literature, while providing other students opportunities to explore different styles in a small-group setting. One student, for example, who has a strong artistic strength, but a reading weakness, gained confidence in her interpretations and understandings of the novel through this literature experience.

Throughout this section of the unit, students supplemented these discussions with a variety of knowledge application activities designed to help review the information gleaned during the literature circles. These activities were based on Tomlinson's (1995) student-centered model of differentiation requiring varying approaches to content, process, and product. These activities were structured so that students could sample the kinds of strengths and interests that would be the focus of the second part of the unit. Some of these activities were assigned to all members of a group, and some were left for students to select and pursue independently as they progressed through their novels. These activities included developing "treasure" maps of characters' journeys, creating characters' résumés for the major tasks in the books, making shopping lists and budgets for characters, creating characters' postcards home from various key points in the novels, and matching events in the novel to the tracks on the *Fantasia* CD.

The group that read Lloyd Alexander's *The Black Cauldron* had to deal with the interactions of more than a dozen characters. Activities included creating Web pages for each main character, reenacting and expanding upon the opening council meeting, and delivering eulogies for a fallen hero. Each of these activities was done in first person with all students assuming the role of one of the main characters. These activities paralleled a larger open-ended problem that would become the central focus of one of the groups in the second part of the unit.

During this section of the unit, groups met 3 times a week for 5 weeks to read and discuss their books. During these first 5 weeks, all students read another fantasy book for their choice reading. Many of the students elected to read other books from the original list, which encouraged dialogue about these texts with their peers in that fantasy book group. Each student also created a computer-generated "Fantasy Newspaper" based on the events in the novels. These included a news article, advertisement, and an illustration, and other components, such as editorials, features, or second news articles, were decided upon in individualized conferences between teachers and students.

After completing their novels, students regrouped for culminating projects based on their preferred learning styles and interests. Each project was presented as an open-ended problem that students would solve by using their new insight into the content and genre (see Appendix C for a list of projects). Students rank ordered their project preferences. In assigning groups, classroom teachers considered these rankings along with input from the group leader from the first part of the unit and their own assessment of the students. All students received one of their top three choices. Once students received their groupings, they "threw themselves into" an intense hour-and-a-half session of work. Students worked cooperatively and devoted about 3 hours a week to this project over a 3-week period.

A culminating "Fantasy Finale" took place in the learning center, which was intended to allow students to showcase their projects and reinforce their collective understanding of all the different factors that comprise the fantasy genre. It was an unbelievable experience to observe how students applied the same concepts in very different ways.

The music group chose to explore the genre of fantasy through a combination of writing and listening activities. Initially, the teacher leading the group played a variety of musical selections (without words) ranging from classical, to country, to recognizable radio hits. This activity encouraged the group to talk about the mood and atmosphere generated by music. All students were encouraged to select a piece of music that appealed to them from a library of CDs. Students generated fantasy ideas that matched their music selections and began to think about possible settings, plots, and characters. They then wrote a fantasy story to accompany their musical selection. The students who displayed a talent for music were inspired and able to transfer their musical strengths into writing. For some, different instruments represented different characters, more subtle shifts in key or notes represented an escalation in events, and connections appeared throughout their writing.

A technology group created an interactive Web site, which included "home pages" for several teams of fantasy characters, each of which had strengths and concomitant weaknesses. Another page showed maps of four regions of a fantastic realm. Readers of the site selected a team that would have to rescue three princesses. Success and direction of the quest depended on the paths chosen through the lands and the talents of the chosen teams. This group moved at an accelerated rate and met more frequently.

The biggest surprises in terms of quality of outcomes came from the "Fantasy Habitat," "Fantasy in Action," and "Fantasy Board Games" groups. Students in the games group focused on their mathematical talents as they connected to literature. One pair of students chose to focus on the otherworldly characters found in fantasy books. Each character selected had particular attributes that enabled them to move in very specific ways around a game board. For example, some characters "flew" ahead in sets of five, some went alternately forward then backward, and some were methodical and direct in their progression. There were alternate and overlapping paths through the game board for air-, land-, or water-based creatures. The partnership then had to design a game board that allowed for each character to have a reasonably fair chance of winning the game, requiring use of percentages, probability, and statistics. Several original characters had to be discarded after tests of the game showed them to have an unfair advantage or disadvantage; specific directions on game squares also had to be developed and edited.

Conclusion

Two goals are central to units of this nature. The first is to help all the students set high-level academic challenges, and the second is to provide a learning environment that supports their meeting these challenges according to their particular creative and academic strengths. To accomplish these goals, we turned to the literature in problem solving and gifted education.

According to the problem-solving literature, across academic fields (Wineburg, 1991; Zeitz, 1994), mastering content is only part of the requisite for solving complex problems; students also need to know the structures (or schemas) pertinent to organizing the content into novel solutions. Expert problem solvers build solutions over time by making connections between content and structure (Bereiter, Burtis, & Scardamalia, 1988; McCutchen, 1986; Smith, 1995). Thus, we first decided what content students would need to know (e.g., the conflict in each book, ways in which specific character traits affect the plots) and then what characteristics are particular to the genre (e.g., the kinds of characters found in the fantasy, enchanted settings). The first part of the unit focused on learning these two aspects of knowledge. The second part stressed integrating these aspects to solve open-ended problems.

The unit was also based on a broadened conception of giftedness (Renzulli, 1998; Renzulli & Reis, 2002) that focuses on many kinds of aptitudes, talents, and potentials for learning that exists in school populations. The gifted literature provided guidelines for offering students a variety of opportunities to work together according to commonality in ability, interests, learning style, and preference for various modes of expression.

In short, in the first part of the unit, teachers provided opportunities that helped all the students in the grade master the content according to their own abilities and interests while introducing them to various modes of expression. Once students were familiar with content and structures, the second part of the unit asked them to apply this knowledge to solve problems (e.g., present a fantasy story through movement to music). Problems were structured so that students could work in a mode of expression and at a level of abstraction with which they felt the most comfortable. Graphic, dramatic, artistic, technological, spatial, and dance were considered in addition to traditional written and spoken expression styles. In each case, students applied their knowledge of fantasy according to their individual strengths and interests.

All students are capable of manifesting higher levels of performance if they can learn and apply content in a way that matches their strengths. This holds true whether the students exhibit their gifts in typical "schoolhouse" settings, need special support to exhibit their superior potential, or simply have a particular strength within their unique profile of talents and interests. Therefore, our goal was to develop a unit that increased challenges for all students and promoted an atmosphere of excellence and creativity. We encouraged all students to learn and apply information and structures according to their individual strengths and interests.

References

Bereiter, C., Burtis, P. J., & Scardamalia, M. (1988). Cognitive operations in constructing main points in written composition. *Journal of Memory and Language, 27,* 261–278.

Chi, M. T. H., Hutchinson, J. E., & Robin, A. F. (1989). How influences about novel domain-related concepts can be constrained by structured knowledge. *Merrill-Palmer Quarterly, 35*(1), 27–62.

Daniels, H. (1994). *Literature circles: Voice and choice in the student-centered classroom.* New York: Stenhouse.

McCutchen, D. (1986). Domain knowledge and linguistic knowledge in the development of writing ability. *Journal of Memory and Language, 24,* 431–444.

Renzulli, J. S. (1998). The three-ring concept of giftedness. In S. M. Baum, S. M. Reis, & L. R. Maxfield (Eds.), *Nurturing the gifts and talents of primary grade students* [Electronic version]. Mansfield Center, CT: Creative Learning Press. Retrieved November 12, 2002, from http:// www.sp.uconn.edu/~nrcgt/ sem/semart13.html

Renzulli, J. S., & Reis, S. M. (2002). *What is schoolwide enrichment? And how do gifted programs relate to total school improvement?* Retrieved February 9, 2002, from http://www. sp.uconn.edu/~nrcgt/sem/whatisem.html

Smith, K. J. (1995). *The developmental influences of content knowledge and linguistic knowledge on experts' and novices' construction of expository text.* Unpublished doctoral dissertation, Columbia University, New York.

Tomlinson, C. (1995). *How to differentiate instruction in mixed-ability classrooms.* Alexandria, VA: Association for Supervision and Curriculum Development.

Tomlinson, C. (1999). *The differentiated classroom: Responding to the needs of all learners.* Alexandria, VA: Association for Supervision and Curriculum Development.

Winebrenner, S. (2001). *Teaching gifted kids in the regular classroom.* Minneapolis, MN: Free Spirit.

Wineburg, S. S. (1991). Historical problem solving: A study of cognitive processes used in the evaluation of documentary and pictorial evidence. *Journal of Educational Psychology, 83,* 73–87.

Zeitz, C. (1994). Expert-novice differences in memory, abstraction, and reasoning in the domain of literature. *Cognition and Instruction, 12,* 277–312.

Appendix A
Fantasy Book Groups

Please order these books in choice of preference from 1 to 6, with 1 being your first choice and 6 being your last choice. If you've already read one of the books, please cross it out (on the line). Please realize that, based on interest and availability, you may not get your first choice.

_____   *Seven Day Magic*
           Five students find magic when they check out an old, shabby book.

_____ *The Last of the Really Great Whangdoodles*
With Professor Savant as their guide, three children
travel on an odyssey to the Whangdoodles

_____ *The Folk Keeper*
A young girl, in charge of guarding the "Folk," dis-
covers who she really is.

_____ *The Lion, the Witch, and the Wardrobe*
An exciting journey into another world.

_____ *Ella Enchanted*
Ella is under a spell that makes her have to obey
commands. Will she ever break free?

_____ *The Black Cauldron*
A King Arthur-like quest story filled with danger
and adventure.

Appendix B
Sample Discussion Questions for *The Folk Keeper*

1. How is Corin's reaction to the Folk unusual?
2. What do you think is happening with Corin's power?
3. Why does the author choose to focus on Corin's physical
   appearance?
4. Which character do you identify with in the story, and what
   qualities do they have that are realistic? What qualities are
   fantastic?
5. Where do you think the Folk go during the day?

Appendix C
Fantasy Groups

Join with other students who share your interests and talents!
Please rank your choices in order from 1 to 7, with 1 being your
first choice and 7 being your last choice.

_____   *Write Your Own Fantasy Story*
Create a story using the elements of fantasy.

_____   *Fantasy in Action*
Present a fantasy story through movement to music.

_____   *Fantasy Music*
Select and arrange songs to accompany a fantasy story.

_____   *Create a Fantasy Habitat*
Where might a fantasy creature live?

_____   *Design a Fantasy Board Game*
From start to finish, take your players on an amazing journey.

_____   *Scenes from a Fantasy*
Readers' theater comes to life!

_____   *Technology*
Explore the world of fantasy by creating a PowerPoint presentation, HyperStudio project, or Web site.

section three

Classroom Management

chapter 8

Cluster Grouping Elementary Gifted Students in the Regular Classroom

a teacher's perspective

by **Kevin M. Teno**

ith cluster grouping, all gifted students at a grade level are assigned to one classroom because of similar learning needs. Typically, these students are assigned to a general education teacher who has an interest or specific training in instructing gifted students. The other students assigned in the classroom are of mixed ability.

According to Hoover, Sayler, and Feldhusen (1993), the major purpose of cluster grouping is to allow identified gifted students to receive all of their instruction within the regular classroom. Such a strategy is considered to be less disruptive than when students are "pulled out" to receive services. Hoover et al. also noted that cluster grouping allows students to receive instruction from one teacher, rather than from several teachers who infrequently collaborate with each other about student progress.

With the current trend in education to include all students within the general education classroom, greater collaboration between gifted education specialists and classroom teachers is needed to improve education for all students. The general education teacher's delivery of services must include a systemic strategy that assists in meeting the specific needs of gifted students who, for the most part, spend the majority of their school day in the general education classroom. The gifted education specialist has an important role in serving as a resource for classroom teachers, as well as assisting with curricular modifications in the general education classroom.

While collaboration is indeed a positive strategy, many general education teachers have expressed some professional concerns about the burden of time placed upon them. For example, the general education teachers are concerned that, not only are they required to make modifications for special education students, but they must also provide appropriate curricular options for gifted students on a daily basis (Coleman, 1995). As a result of these concerns, the educational strategy of clustering is increasingly identified as a solution that lessens the burden on general education teachers and addresses the needs of gifted students (Parpart, 1995). Since all children have a right to learn every day in class, the strategy of cluster grouping provides "the same opportunities for the gifted that all other kids experience: consistent opportunities for learning challenges" (Winebrenner, 1992, p. 127). It is this challenge that educational programs must address in providing differentiated services for gifted students within the general education classroom.

This chapter will examine cluster grouping as a viable option for meeting the needs of gifted and talented students. It will also examine the strengths and weaknesses of cluster grouping from the perspective of teachers who have implemented this strategy in an elementary school district.

Cluster Grouping as a Viable Option

According to the literature, cluster grouping can be successful in meeting the needs of gifted students in the regular classroom. Several researchers in the field of gifted education have identified a number of positive aspects of establishing cluster groups that make it a viable option.

One advantage of cluster grouping for gifted students is that it provides an opportunity to be grouped with intellectual peers.

Hoover et al. (1993) concluded that gifted students should have the opportunity to interact with like-ability peers for intellectual, social, and emotional support. According to Winebrenner and Devlin (1996), cluster grouping allows gifted students to feel less isolated and less stressed because they are clustered with other students of similar abilities. Winebrenner (1992) also noted that cluster grouping provides gifted students with the opportunity to select more challenging activities and produce more in-depth and quality products because they are working with others within the classroom environment instead of working alone.

There are advantages for the regular students, as well. When a cluster grouping model is implemented, "there may be a positive effect on the achievement and identification of all students, not just those identified and placed in the cluster for high-ability students" (Gentry, 1996, p. 11). Gentry also concluded that cluster grouping allows the highest achieving students to be removed from other classrooms, thereby allowing new leaders to emerge. Hoover et al. (1993) noted that high-ability students who are not formally identified could be included with the cluster group for educational opportunities in their areas of strength.

According to some researchers, the use of cluster grouping also offers a financial advantage to school districts. Parpart (1995) reported that cluster grouping requires little additional money to support. With the exception of teacher training, no additional funds are needed for its implementation. "Cluster grouping provides gifted students with something their parents have always been told the district could never afford: a full-time gifted program" (Winebrenner, 1992, p. 129).

Negative Aspects of Cluster Grouping

While the literature indicates that cluster grouping is effective, it also points to some limitations that ought to be addressed.

One of the most prominent criticisms of cluster grouping is that it is simply another word for tracking. However, Winebrenner (1992) concluded that cluster grouping and tracking are different:

> In a tracking system, all students are grouped by ability for much of the school day, and students tend to remain in the same track throughout their years in school. In cluster grouping, only the gifted are grouped together in their areas of strength, because they learn better that way. Students of all other ability levels are grouped heterogeneously, because present research indicates that this is the best arrangement for them. (p. 126)

According to Kulik and Kulik (1991), gifted students learn better when they are cluster grouped according to their areas of strength. Winebrenner and Devlin (1996) concluded that cluster grouping allows gifted students to learn together while avoiding permanent placement for all other students.

One problem that may detract from the effectiveness of cluster grouping is the selection and training of cluster teachers. Parpart (1995) concluded that the teacher who is responsible for the instruction of the cluster group should have a desire and be qualified to teach them. She also noted that, if students are clustered, but instructional strategies are not changed, then cluster grouping could be a disservice to students. According to Hoover et al. (1993), teachers need training in working with gifted students and curriculum differentiation. Winebrenner and Devlin (1996) determined that the success of the cluster-grouping strategy depends on how well the general education classroom teachers are trained in curriculum compacting, accelerating the pace of instruction, providing enrichment, and incorporating students' interests into their independent study projects. It is important to cluster group gifted students with a teacher who has a specific background in gifted education and who has the skills necessary to differentiate the curriculum.

Beyond having trained teachers, another barrier to the successful implementation of cluster grouping is the amount of work required of general education classroom teachers (Hoover et al., 1993). Schuler (1997) noted that, with the increased responsibility of the cluster group, teachers' workload increased and they did not have enough collaboration time. Rogers (1991) indicated that teachers need to be given adequate time to plan and provide appropriate instruction for the cluster group.

Coleman (1995) concluded that the cluster teacher should consult with the gifted education specialist who has training in meeting the needs of gifted students. Furthermore, "This specialist should help plan curriculum compacting, select and procure appropriate materials, team teach lessons, and facilitate independent student projects" (Coleman, p. 39).

The responsibilities placed on general education teachers are tremendous. In addition, the needs of the students who come to school each day reflect a diversity of backgrounds that offers a challenge to educators. Teachers must continually work to address the needs of all students, including the gifted. As these students present challenges, there is a need to provide alternative ways of serving them.

The next section of this chapter examines cluster grouping as one possible solution to meeting the needs of gifted students within one general education classroom.

A Pilot Study

As a gifted education specialist in a suburban elementary school district, the issue of cluster grouping became increasingly important to me in my teaching assignment. Since my professional responsibilities included more than one elementary building and the gifted students were scattered among several general education classrooms, I was concerned about the effectiveness of their educational services.

One of these concerns was that there was a lack of communication between me and the general education teachers. Another concern was the strong indication that general education teachers needed assistance and preparation in modifying the curriculum to meet the needs of gifted students. From my point of view, these concerns made it necessary to explore alternative methods of delivering services to gifted students, including the option of cluster grouping. I therefore planned, implemented, and evaluated a cluster-grouping pilot program to examine how cluster grouping could be used as an option for gifted students and how general education teachers responded.

Demographics

At the time of this pilot study, I was employed in a school system located in a suburban area in central Iowa. There were two elementary buildings serving approximately 608 students in grades K–4. The children involved in the experimental cluster group were identified gifted children who were placed in one heterogeneous fourth-grade classroom.

The total fourth-grade population was 116 students divided among five sections. Seven of these students were identified as gifted: four in reading, two in mathematics, and one in general intellectual aptitude. The general education classroom teacher and the gifted education specialist were responsible for making content modifications for these identified students.

The seven gifted and talented students were identified for the gifted cluster prior to entry into the fourth grade based on the following criteria: teacher nominations, behavioral observations, student portfolios, and the Iowa Test of Basic Skills with cutoff scores of 90% or above in one or more of the following areas: vocabulary, reading, language, mathematics concepts, mathematics problems, mathematics total, and core composite.

The students were identified for the gifted and talented program in the areas of general intellectual ability and specific academic aptitude. General intellectual ability refers to students who can learn at a faster pace, master higher levels of content, and handle abstract concepts at a significantly higher level than expected given their chronological age and experience. Specific academic aptitude refers to those students who have exceptionally high achievement or potential and a high degree of interest in a specific field of study.

The Program Environment

The elementary gifted program for this school district is comprised of five service levels. These service levels assist parents and teachers in designing an individually differentiated program based on the strengths and talents of each student.

At the first level, Advocacy, the gifted education specialist aids identified students in individualizing their programs, thus enabling students to reach their academic potential. Both cognitive and affective needs are addressed at this level. Components of Advocacy include (a) conducting individual interviews and assessments to diagnose student needs and learning styles; (b) writing a detailed PEP (Personalized Education Plan) for every identified student with parent, student, and staffing input; (c) implementing and monitoring the PEP; (d) communicating with parents, students, staff, and community on in-servicing, programming, planning, and progress; and (e) representing the student's best interests—problem solving and advocating for appropriate educational programming.

The second level is Special Opportunities. At this level, special events and opportunities are offered to gifted and talented students and other highly interested able students. Special Opportunities at the elementary level may include activities such as Math Olympiads, National Language Arts Olympiad, Stock Market Game, News Bowl USA, and other activities based on students' needs and interests.

The third service level is Extension of the Regular Curriculum. At this service level, the general education teacher and the gifted education specialist work together to provide opportunities for talent development and enrichment through the regular classroom to benefit all students. Team teaching, extended learning contracts, and resourcing are used at this level.

The fourth service level is Modification of the Regular Curriculum. At this level, the gifted education specialist and the general education teacher collaborate with parents to create a plan of instruction and implementation as designed on the PEP. Modifications may include compacting, acceleration, and enrichment.

The fifth service level offers a Pull-In Class, where the gifted students are removed from the general education classroom and meet with the gifted education specialist for special instruction in working on projects in their areas of academic and general intellectual abilities. Pull-In students are included in this plan because they benefit from both individualized instruction and interaction with like-ability peers. The gifted education specialist works with these students on developing process skills that will lead directly to self-directed learning and independent study.

Organizational Structure

The ideal delivery option for a cluster group would be for the identified gifted students to receive all of their instruction within the general education classroom. Since my teaching assignment includes two elementary buildings with five grade levels, the ideal cluster grouping set-up was not feasible. Therefore, for 3 days a week, I was assigned to the elementary building that contained the identified cluster group. The remaining 2 days of the week were spent in the other elementary school building.

To ensure greater continuity between the regular education program and the gifted program, the cluster teacher and I met once each week for a minimum of 30 minutes. During this time, we had the opportunity to select materials, gather resources, and also plan differentiated activities for the week. The planning time together was also a perfect opportunity for monitoring the progress of the gifted students.

Because the identified students were cluster grouped, I had the opportunity to work with these students for 2 days a week in the areas of both integrated language arts and math. Depending upon the activities planned for the week, I was able to work with the cluster group in either the general education classroom or the gifted education classroom. The cluster teacher provided differentiated services to the cluster group during the remaining 3 days of the week.

Modifications for the identified students in the area of integrated language arts included higher level trade books, higher order thinking skills, and creative writing. Differentiated activities for the identified mathematics students included logic, geometry, problem solving, and extensions of the regular classroom curriculum.

In addition to working with the identified students on the core subject areas of integrated language arts and math, I met with the cluster group in a Pull-In Class for approximately 75 minutes per week. The focus of this class was on using a variety of models and teaching strategies that were effective for gifted learners. Curricular elements for the Pull-In Class included (a) getting the students oriented to the program options; (b) building independent, self-directed learning skills; (c) conducting

Please answer each of the following questions on the cluster grouping strategy.

1. What role does curriculum modifications play in your classroom?

2. What do you see as the advantages of the cluster grouping strategy?

3. What do you see as the disadvantages of the cluster grouping strategy?

4. What would you change to meet the needs of gifted students in your classroom?

Figure 8.1. **Cluster grouping survey**

group and independent studies in specific content; and (d) producing quality student products and presentations.

Evaluation of the Program

At the end of the first year of implementing the cluster-grouping program, I used my own reflections, conferences with teachers, observations in both the general education cluster classroom and the resource room, and a survey of the fourth-grade general education classroom teachers to evaluate the use of the cluster grouping strategy (see Figure 8.1).

Positive Implications

After 1 year of implementing the strategy of cluster grouping and on the basis of my survey results, I discovered benefits to gifted students, the cluster teacher, and regular students. The general education teachers indicated that clustering allowed the gifted students to work together in groups for intellectual stimulation and social support. The cluster teacher also revealed that she provided these students with more challenging activities. In addition, I observed that the cluster group demonstrated a new enthusiasm for learning by working at a pace that was more conducive to individual rates of learning.

There also proved to be advantages for the cluster teacher. First of all, the cluster teacher reported that cluster grouping allows one general education teacher to design modified activities instead of having several general education teachers each design activities separately for gifted students. The cluster teacher also noted that clustering allowed the general education teacher more individualized time to work with other students in that classroom. Furthermore, she reported an increase in communication and support between the cluster teacher and the gifted education specialist.

Interestingly, cluster grouping also seemed to benefit regular students. While the cluster grouping provided the gifted students with a modified curriculum, exposed them to higher level questioning strategies, and presented them with more hands-on learning activities, it also significantly raised the standards and expectations for the whole class. In fact, in some cases, a number of nonidentified high-ability students were also included in certain activities based upon their interests and abilities.

Negative Implications

There were a few pitfalls that hindered the successful implementation of the cluster-grouping strategy in this particular pilot. First, with the increased responsibility of the cluster group, the cluster teacher indicated that extra time was needed to prepare materials and plan instruction for this group. To help minimize the problems associated with time, she suggested that the cluster teacher be given more time to prepare lessons and materials for the cluster group, as well as to collaborate with the gifted and talented specialist in order to assist with providing appropriate services for gifted students.

Second, noncluster teachers indicated that cluster grouping allowed few, if any, chances for each classroom to enjoy gifted students modeling for others. Winebrenner (1992) noted that it is important to ensure other high-ability students are included in nonclustered classrooms so they have opportunities to serve as positive role-models and also become new leaders in classes that no longer contain identified gifted students.

A final concern was one noncluster teacher's belief that cluster grouping tracks students. To address this particular criticism, it is imperative to educate the staff, parents, and students about the research relative to cluster grouping. Winebrenner (1992) recommended providing staff development for all teachers. She also suggested that rotating the staff every year or two helps to send a message to parents that there are many teachers who can provide appropriate educational opportunities for gifted students.

Conclusions and Recommendations

My examination of the literature related to cluster grouping as a strategy for meeting the needs of gifted students in the context of the total school environment convinced me of its feasibility. My implementation of the strategy through a pilot study provided a unique opportunity to test that feasibility. These two activities have led me to reach some tentative conclusions concerning the effectiveness of cluster grouping, as well as some recommendations for the improvement and expansion of this strategy in the gifted education classroom.

First of all, the reviewed literature reflected a current trend in education that strongly focuses on a desire to improve instruction for all students. Therefore, it seems evident that gifted education programs should interface their services with general education programs in order to implement a schoolwide collaboration process that focuses on school improvement. The strategy of cluster grouping gifted students within the general education classroom and the resulting modification of the curriculum can be one effective component in restructuring schools to improve classroom instruction for all children, including the gifted and talented.

Second, the reviewed literature showed that collaboration and proper planning increases the likelihood of success in cluster grouping. Collaboration of the cluster teacher with the gifted education specialist is important in both the planning and the implementation of instructional strategies to meet the needs of these students. Through a collaborative effort, the cluster teacher's methods of teaching are enhanced, and gifted students are provided with more comprehensive services, rather than programs limited to relatively infrequent short periods of time when they are "pulled in" to work with the gifted education specialist. My pilot study also reaffirmed that collaboration is an important ingredient in the success of cluster grouping. The cluster teacher and I benefited from exposure to each other's training and experience while working together as a team to create an environment that provided learning opportunities for all students to become successful learners in the general education classroom.

Third, from the reviewed literature, it became apparent that the selection of the cluster teacher is critical to the success of cluster grouping. This professional should have an interest and a desire to work with gifted students, rather than having the cluster group assigned by an administrator. The cluster teacher should be provided with the proper training, resources, and support needed to address the characteristics of gifted students, who require curricular modifications that extend beyond what is provided in the general education classroom. The cluster teacher must be willing to dedicate a proportionate amount of classroom time to providing appropriate learning opportunities for the cluster group. My pilot study reaffirmed that the selection of the cluster teacher is important to the cluster-grouping process. In working with the cluster teacher, I observed that she was willing to devote extra planning time and classroom instructional time to provide appropriate learning opportunities for the cluster group.

Fourth, the planning, implementation, and evaluation of this study have convinced me that the cluster-grouping strategy does not need, nor should it be designed, to replace the current gifted program. The value of this approach lies in its implementation as a supplement to current gifted programs and its flexibility as a strategy that can be modified to meet the goals and objectives of other districts that may have more than one building.

My work with teachers, parents, and administrators also led me to conclude that, while clustering is successful, it cannot stand alone. Teachers are faced with the difficult task of providing differentiated instruction for 25 to 30 students in a classroom. Therefore, it is imperative that the general education teachers work collaboratively with the gifted education specialist to implement the cluster-grouping strategy and make daily modifications to the curriculum in order to meet the needs of our most capable students. In addition, administrators should provide both general education teachers and cluster teachers with ongoing staff development about strategies designed to meet the unique needs of gifted students. These strategies, in turn, may well benefit nonidentified students.

References

Coleman, M. R. (1995). The importance of cluster grouping. *Gifted Child Today, 18*(1), 38–40.

Gentry, M. (1996, Spring). Total school cluster grouping: An investigation of achievement and identification of elementary school students. *The National Research Center on the Gifted and Talented Newsletter,* 8–11.

Hoover, S. M., Sayler, M., & Feldhusen, J. F. (1993). Cluster grouping of gifted students at the elementary level. *Roeper Review, 16,* 13–15.

Kulik, J. A., & Kulik, C. C. (1991). Ability grouping and gifted students. In N. Colangelo & G. A. Davis (Eds.), *Handbook of gifted education* (pp. 178–196). Needham Heights, MA: Allyn and Bacon.

Parpart, M. L. (1995). *Cluster grouping students in the regular classroom: Barriers to success.* Charlottesville: Curry School of Education, University of Virginia. (ERIC Document Reproduction Service No. ED384593)

Rogers, K. B. (1991). Grouping the gifted and talented: Questions and answers. *Roeper Review, 16,* 8–12.

Schuler, P. A. (1997, Winter). Cluster grouping coast to coast. *The National Research Center on the Gifted and Talented Newsletter,* 11–15.

Winebrenner, S. (1992). *Teaching gifted kids in the regular classroom.* Minneapolis, MN: Free Spirit.

Winebrenner, S., & Devlin, B. (1996). *Cluster grouping fact sheet: How to provide full-time services for gifted students on reasonable budgets.* Brooklyn, MI: Phantom Press.

chapter 9

The Room Meeting For G/T Students in an Inclusion Classroom

by John Feldhusen *and* Hazel Feldhusen

ifted and talented children have great potential at the primary level for self-direction and independent study in the regular classroom, and they can work effectively with children of low and average ability to make the regular classroom a place for creative and productive learning in the basic subject matters. We developed a system of individualized instruction for second grade (Feldhusen, 1993) that has been applied in all the different elementary grades and found to be an effective system for actively involving the gifted and talented as a cluster and as individuals in the regular classroom. The children work at their own individual achievement levels in reading, writing, and mathematics. One major aspect of the system is the weekly classroom meeting in which all children participate, but the gifted and talented are expected to take a leadership role.

Children often take a completely passive view toward classroom operations and assume that the teacher has total control and decides all that goes on in the classroom. Instead, we wanted to teach children that they should assume some responsibility for what goes on in the classroom and for the development of new ideas to enhance classroom operations and activities. The gifted and talented, according to Coleman and Cross (2002), have great potential to be actively involved in and responsible for classroom operations.

We developed a plan for classroom organization for grades 1–6 and implemented individualized instruction, with the children writing daily learning agreements concerning the topics, order, and time they would devote to the different areas of the curriculum. Individual learning centers were set up in the basic curricular areas. There was a reading corner and library with small rockers, an area where the children were seated and working in small groups of three or four, and an area where the gifted and talented were clustered to work together some of the time (but also mixed much of the time). The gifted children were never labeled as such, but were identified by intelligence tests with quotients above 135 and achievement test scores in math and reading above the 95th percentile, which followed identification guidelines for Indiana (Adams-Byers, 1998).

In this article, we will discuss the method of classroom meetings that were used to involve all the children in operations of the classroom and to give them a feeling that they could influence the success or failure of their experiences in the classroom. We will comment on the role of gifted and talented youth throughout this article.

Weekly Meetings

The weekly meetings were used over a period of 12 years and found to be very productive in improving classroom operations, building classroom morale, and promoting creative classroom activities. The meetings were about 25 to 35 minutes in length and focused on identifying problems and advancing solutions and new ideas to improve classroom learning. During personal contacts, we communicated to the gifted and talented students that we had high expectations for their participation in these classroom meetings.

At the beginning of the year, certain rules were established. This was not the time nor place to air personal grievances against other children, nor was it the time for tattle-tailing. New, high-powered, and creative ideas were welcome. If anyone suggested a new development for the classroom, he or she should also be prepared to work at implementing it. If someone identified a classroom problem, he or she should also be ready to think about possible solutions. Furthermore, whenever someone did not know a big word that was used—and this was done purposely, especially for gifted and talented children—he or she was to ask to have the word written on the board and explained or to go to the dictionary in the classroom library and look it up.

The classroom meeting began on Tuesday of the second week of the school year right after lunch, with the teacher serving as chairperson or leader for the first month and then student volunteers serving as chair for the rest of the year. One of the early meetings was devoted to brainstorming guidelines for student volunteer leaders. The children produced many good ideas that they were able to use in future weekly meetings. Several of the early volunteer leaders were gifted and talented children. Once they had volunteered to lead, a meeting was scheduled with the teacher to discuss their plans for the meeting and to develop a preliminary agenda.

Ideas and Projects

Over the period of 12 years conducting room meetings, many good ideas were introduced and developed. At one meeting, a boy, talented on the piano, offered to play the piano for some group singing. The children loved this, and it became a regular feature of the room, with all the children singing at the top of their voices. Of course, other musical instruments were also featured, including violins and flutes.

On yet another occasion, a gifted girl said she had heard from her dad that the great pilot Amelia Earhart had once been a professor at Purdue University. She suggested that we have a special classroom report on Amelia Earhart and volunteered to lead the effort. With a team of four volunteers, the project went forward. With a mother's help on a Saturday, they went to the

Purdue library to supplement what they could find in our school library. There they found a lot of information and memorabilia about Amelia Earhart's time as a professor at Purdue, and they were able to get some pictures copied for the report. All this effort led to an excellent oral report involving all of the team members. Several of the gifted children had already read a book or two about Amelia Earhart, and they contributed a great deal more during the discussion that followed. The entire effort was a good, challenging, and productive experience for several talented and precocious second graders.

One idea, advanced by a gifted boy, was to have mailboxes for all the children and the teacher. He and a group of several other children went on to build the mailboxes with milk cartons. At a later meeting, a girl suggested that the children should send notes complementing one another for good, courteous, and creative behaviors. Many children later reported that they had received such notes and were thrilled to get them.

At one of the meetings, a child asked whether students could send notes to the teacher when they had problems with learning tasks. That was a great idea that was encouraged. Some children found it easier to send notes about problems that they were having than to talk to their teacher about them.

The mailboxes were also an excellent means of communication to the teacher about learning problems. While some of the notes were simple expressions of liking the teacher or enthusiasm for the ball game at recess, some noted a need for help with reading words or the current mathematics lessons. The volume of notes grew throughout the year.

A gifted boy and girl together sent a note saying they wanted to learn long division (this is early in second grade). They were given a fourth-grade math book and told they could study the section on long division and the teacher would meet with them later. About an hour later in the meeting with teacher, it was clear that they had already mastered long division and were very proud of their accomplishment. There were many similar messages, especially from gifted and talented children, asking for opportunities to study advanced topics while the less able and lower achievers most often asked for help with difficulties they were experiencing with lessons. Since there was much emphasis on individualized learning, this was a great help in implementing the overall classroom system.

The room meetings often turned to major events of the day, which were most often noted by one or more of the gifted and talented cluster. Having heard that a professor of veterinary medicine had received a grant of $1 million, they wondered if that was all to care for cats and dogs. In the discussion that followed, one of the children, whose father was a Purdue professor, told the group that the professor did research on large animals so he could help other veterinarians treat such animals. Several children then told about research their fathers were doing.

As an outgrowth of that discussion, several children suggested they would like to do a TV news show and videotape it. Five children (including three gifted) volunteered for that project: one to be the newscaster, one the weather person, one the sports announcer, one the videocamera operator, and one the news director, who would write copy for the announcers. It took the group a week to get organized, and they produced a fine show. The videotape was first viewed by the class and then loaned to individual children to take home for viewing with their parents.

There was much effort to get all the children involved in the room meetings and to contribute ideas. However, a problem noted by many teachers of the gifted is their high level of verbalizing and dominance in discussions. Thus, the class was often broken down into little groups of four to six to discuss and brainstorm solutions to ideas or problems that had been proposed in the room meeting. The gifted cluster consisted of four to six children each year, and they constituted one of the room meeting groups.

One idea, brought up in the room meetings, was to have a talent show the class might perform for other classes. In small groups, they settled on some general areas they would have to consider, such as how to identify all the talents we had in the room, what talents would be included in the show, how to stage the show, whether parents should be invited, and so forth. It ended up taking several meetings of work in the small groups before they could pull it all together to prepare for the show. The gifted and talented cluster took on the task of identifying the children's talents and what could all be included.

The show went well, but a number of room meetings were devoted to discussing emerging problems, new ideas for the show, and the staging. Finally, the show was performed for parents and all the primary grades. There were gymnasts, impersonators, dancers, clowns, and musicians galore. Some of the performances involved several children at once. They closed with a group sing involving the audience. At the end, the applause was noisy and the children took a well-earned bow. In the next room meeting, they did their own evaluation to identify what went well and what fell short.

Perhaps the dramatic and creative things that were brought forth and dealt with in room meetings have been highlighted too much in this article, so it should be added that every meeting involved some attention to problems with classroom operations, lessons, and learning: waiting in line too long at the pencil sharpener, difficulties with our cluster seating arrangement, how to get more time for library, missing cards in the reading kit, children who stay too long in the reading center, or things missing from the science study center. The children would often be able to think of good solutions to the problems someone had brought up.

The room meeting offers splendid opportunities for both the gifted and talented and all children to participate in operations of the classroom, to advance their best and creative ideas, to identify and solve problems, and to advance their own learning. It works well in all primary grades, but it takes time to help all children learn how to participate and profit from meetings. And, from the teacher's point of view, it is a joy to see children grow and succeed in their capacity to be self-directing and successful contributors to the social milieu in which they live.

Summary

Classroom management can be enhanced and improved a great deal by weekly cooperative class meetings in which gifted and talented children are given opportunities to offer ideas, solutions, and creative insights (Webb & Palincsar, 1996). All children can and should be encouraged to participate and offer ideas, but the advanced thinking skills, creative abilities, and diverse personal and social characteristics of the gifted and talented make them a particularly rich source of ideas for classroom management. These meetings offered good opportunities for children to learn leadership skills, to engage in cooperative learning to enhance their learning of subject matter, and, for the gifted and talented, to master higher level cognitive and social skills.

References

Adams-Byers, J. (1998). *Assessing high-ability students.* Indianapolis: Indiana State Department of Education Gifted/Talented Unit.

Coleman, L. J., & Cross, T. L. (2002). Social-emotional development and the personal experience of giftedness. In K. A. Heller, F. J. Mönks, R. J. Sternberg, & R. F. Subotnik (Eds.), *International handbook of giftedness and talent* (2nd ed., pp. 203–212). New York: Elsevier.

Feldhusen, H. J. (1993). *Individualized teaching of the gifted in the regular classroom.* Buffalo: D.O.K.

Webb, N. M., & Palincsar, A. S. (1996). Group processes in the classroom. In D. C. Berliner & R. C. Calfee (Eds.), *Handbook of educational psychology* (pp. 841–873). New York: Simon and Schuster/ Macmillan.

chapter 10

Four Levels of Learning Centers for Use With Young Gifted Children

by Peggy L. Snowden *and* Linda Garris Christian

*a*lmost every early childhood and many lower primary classrooms, including resource rooms for young gifted children, have at least one learning center. It is now commonplace to see centers in classrooms, particularly those in which the teacher is committed to creating a learning atmosphere based on the principles of constructivism, child-centered learning autonomy, and self-efficacy. Teachers use many different terms to label the "center approach," including "play areas," "learning centers," "work centers," "play centers," and "work stations." In this chapter, these areas will be referred to as "learning centers"; but, no matter what the label, teachers who use this approach in their work with youngsters must carefully plan and implement these centers in order to ensure that quality learning takes place.

We have had years of experience teaching in early childhood programs in the lower primary grades and in self-contained/resource room settings for preschool to second-grade gifted children. Throughout our teaching careers, we arrived (somewhat intuitively and through trial and error) at a four-level system for planning and implementing learning centers:

- Level 1: Teacher-planned/teacher-directed;
- Level 2: Teacher-planned/student-directed;
- Level 3: Student-planned/teacher-directed; and
- Level 4: Student-planned/student-directed.

These levels comprise a hierarchy. The first two levels are typically seen in early childhood classrooms, while the third and fourth levels can more easily be used in naturalistic settings where the children have the ability to plan and direct their own learning with teacher guidance. Thus, students generally become experienced with Level 1 before proceeding to Levels 2, 3, and 4. As soon as possible, teachers should use several levels of play areas/learning centers at the same time. Additionally, the levels proceed from high teacher control/teacher-centered to high student-control/student-centered. The aspects of control and centeredness will be explained in the following sections.

Before giving the specifics of the levels with examples, the philosophical, curricular, and instructional foundations for the levels will be explained. In the age of accountability, teachers must justify and explain what is being implemented in their classrooms. Teachers who have learning centers without understanding the underlying principles may have difficulty supporting their use. While they may believe that centers are best for children, if they cannot justify their use to administration and parents, they may meet with resistance to "just having the children play in centers." When parents and administrators understand the depth of learning taking place, they can be more supportive and appreciative.

Philosophical, Curricular, and Instructional Foundations

Although there may be some slight changes in wording, there are four major schools of educational philosophy with four related curricular models: essentialism (also called idealism), scientific materialism, pragmatism, and existentialism. There are also four major families of instruction: behaviorism, information processing, social, and personal (Joyce, Weil, & Showers, 2003).

Philosophy guides and drives the type of curricular model and instructional family used in a particular school and classroom, whether or not the teacher is consciously aware of it. An individual's philosophy is a belief or system of beliefs about what is truth, what is reality, and what has value, and it is accepted as authoritative; synonyms include *ideology, mental attitude, concept, view,* and *blueprint.* Since *blueprint* is a concrete word, we will use it to help elaborate upon both general philosophy and specific educational philosophy.

Every teacher enters the classroom with an established, but flexible and fluid general philosophy—a blueprint about life. The individual's general philosophy then provides the basis for the educational philosophy he or she adopts.

Essentialism is the most directed, objective philosophy. It states that reality is external and absolute, knowledge is a product of reason, and goodness and value are what God wills. Scientific materialism states that reality is the physical universe, knowledge is relative and objective, and what is good and what has value are the verified natural laws. According to pragmatism, what is real is what is workable and practical; knowledge is derived from what works and is positive; and goodness and value are relative, tentative, and are always in flux. Existentialism is the most mental and subjective philosophy. According to this philosophy, reality is what the individual perceives as real, and it takes place in the mind and is modified by individual bias; knowledge and truth are subjective; and what is good and has value is complete freedom and the ability to choose.

While philosophy defines the framework, the curriculum provides the content, the purpose for an educational program, and the organization (Ornstein & Hunkins, 1993). The curriculum encompasses two main goals: content (subject matter) and process (ways of learning) goals. The organization or the attitudes and actions of those engaged in teaching and learning is guided by philosophy.

The subject-centered curriculum is related to the philosophy of essentialism. The focus is on individual content areas with a high degree of structure and teacher control. The process-centered curriculum is connected to scientific materialism and emphasizes process over product, with a moderate degree of structure and high-to-moderate teacher control. The society-centered model is related to pragmatism. This curricular model is based on society, human problems, social studies, and future trends and issues. There is an informal structure and shared control, and the teacher is a guide and mentor. Existentialism gives rise to the person-centered curriculum, which is highly informal and contains a high degree of student control. It is individualized, emergent, and is based on freedom and choice. Self-development and affective skills are stressed.

Instruction involves the behaviors and activities of the people involved in the act of teaching. Instruction is the delivery system for the curriculum, thus, the four instructional families are related to philosophy and curricular models. Philosophy guides the selected curricular model, which is implemented through a selected instructional family. Just as the philosophies and curricular models are arranged in a loose hierarchy, so too are the instructional families.

The behavioral systems family is rooted in the theory of cybernetics. Behaviorism states that a human being is a self-correcting system and learning is composed of permanent changes of behavior based on action-feedback modification of a behavior loop; thus, learning occurs. Instruction in the behavioral systems family consists of carefully organizing tasks and the feedback structure so that the self-correcting loop can function effectively and efficiently. Programmed instruction, mastery learning (Bloom, 1971; Guskey & Gates, 1986), direct instruction or explicit teaching (Glasser, 1969; Rosenshine, 1986), and active teaching (Good, 1983) are common types of instruction rooted in the behavioral systems family.

The information-processing family takes advantage of the theory that human beings have an inborn drive to make sense of perceptions (i.e., information) by organizing data, generating solutions to perceived problems, and developing schemas and relationships between concepts, as well as using language. Instruction revolves around enhancing and strengthening the processing techniques used to acquire and organize information, developing schemas, using language, problem solving, and thinking creatively. Ausubel's (1963) advance organizers, concept attainment (Bruner, Goodnow, & Austin, 1967), and Bruner's (1960) scientific inquiry are all examples of instructional models based on information-processing.

The social family models stress the importance of synergy, the collective energy that takes place when human beings work in close conjunction and union with each other. The founding premise is that the unification of effort is more efficient and effective. Dewey (1910, 1916) is traditionally considered the driving force behind the democratic approach to education. Dewey (1916) urged educators to organize the entire school system around the democratic model of government, so that students might be active participants in the development and administration of the social system. Group investigation (Thelen, 1960) and cooperative learning (Johnson, Johnson, & Holubec, 1990; Slavin, 1994) are prime examples of social family instruction.

The personal family is based on the principle of individual uniqueness, selfhood, self-awareness, and personal autonomy and responsibility. This family stresses the singularity and distinctiveness of each person's perspective, experiences, and understandings. Nondirective teaching, which developed from the work of psychologist Carl Rogers (1980; Rogers & Freiberg, 1994); synectics (Gordon, 1961); and the classroom meeting (Glasser, 1969) are examples of instruction in the personal family.

The philosophies and instructional families are reflected in the levels of the centers in the following manner. In Level 1, the philosophy of essentialism and the instructional family of behaviorism is the primary focus. For Level 2, scientific materialism and the information-processing family are the main elements present. In Level 3, pragmatism and the social family are reflected. And, in Level 4, existentialism and the personal instructional family are present.

Elements of each philosophy and each instructional family, particularly the social family, are present in each level. There are aspects of socialization in any learning center by its very nature. Figure 10.1 provides a visual picture of the four levels. Figure 10.2 and Figure 10.3 contain concrete examples of how each level might look in a given classroom.

There is as much variety and flexibility in the way the levels can be managed as there are teachers who teach in early childhood pro-

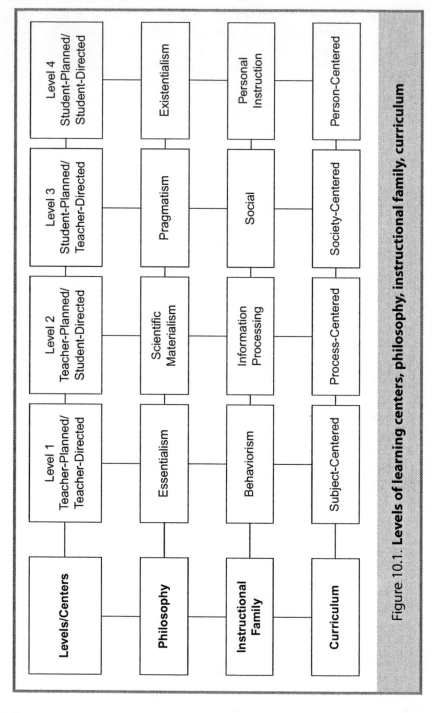

Figure 10.1. **Levels of learning centers, philosophy, instructional family, curriculum**

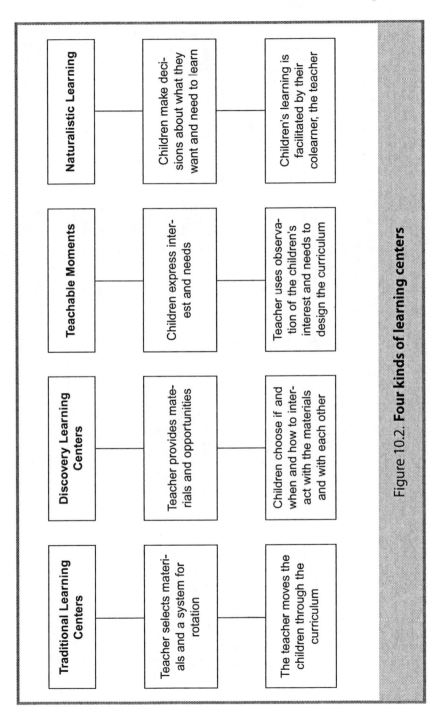

Figure 10.2. **Four kinds of learning centers**

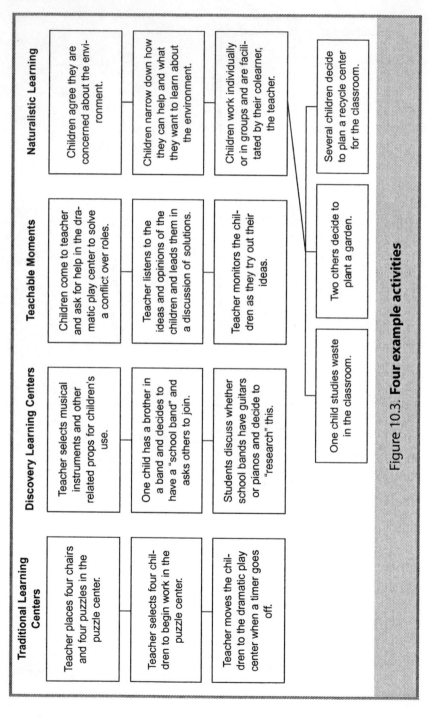

Figure 10.3. **Four example activities**

grams for gifted children. The ideal is to get to the point where all four levels are operating in a classroom at the same time. Teachers adjust and adapt the use of the levels based on assessment of each child, as well as the class as a whole. Observation will provide the basis for decisions about the readiness of each child or small groups of children. Be sure that the children have had lots of experience with the preceding level, and introduce a new level slowly and with plenty of scaffolding (i.e., modeling and support). Attempting to open the year with all four levels at once generally results in chaos and management difficulties, particularly with children who have no prior experience with a center approach.

Level 1

Level 1 is the classic learning center. The teacher provides materials and instructions. Likewise, the teacher has a specific management system and assigns children to centers. Usually there is some sort of rotation. If the teacher uses a name-tag management system, the name tags are hung next to the assigned center and are rotated on a time basis, for example, every 20 minutes. Many early childhood textbooks contain examples of this type of learning center. Real-life examples can be viewed in a majority of developmentally appropriate early childhood classrooms, including self-contained and resource room settings for young gifted children. There is usually an arrangement of typical areas, such as the block area, creative arts area, science table, game area, and home living area. The materials are in place in each area, and, although there is some flexibility in what the children can do, the activities are limited and the teacher chooses what materials are available and the time limit for use of the center.

Level 2

This is the "discovery learning" type of center. The teacher provides materials and has tentative, flexible, and nondirective objectives in mind. Materials are placed in the center, and the teacher lets the children explore or "mess around" with them. Time and movement are much more flexible at this level.

One author has had experiences with rhythm band centers on this level. Instruments were set out, but the children were in charge of what happened in the rhythm band. The blocks from the block center were taken to a large open space in the classroom and used to build a "bandstand." A tape recorder was borrowed from the listening center to make an audio recording of the band. Costumes were obtained from the dramatic play center, and a sign was constructed using materials from the art center.

Level 3

At this level, a student or group of students initiates the center design through an activity or statement of interest. The teacher then takes advantage of this interest, comparable to what is called the "teachable moment."

One author had a perfect opportunity to develop this level of center based on an experience with shadows. While walking to lunch, a child began stepping on the teacher's shadow. A discussion of what he was doing followed with questions about shadows from the child and from the teacher.

After lunch, during rest time, the teacher pulled a storybook that centered on shadows and shared the story with the child. The next day, she arranged a center that would allow him to explore shadows in more detail. She used a small, dark-colored pup tent, two flashlights, and two books to make a reading nook. This prompted more questions and discussion by not only this child, but by four other youngsters.

The next day, the teacher provided an overhead projector, paper, markers, and transparencies in the art center. She also used a shadow puppet story at literacy time, with the materials being placed in the library center later that day.

Over the course of the next few days, five children were consistently interested in the activities provided; almost all the children participated in some of the activities during the course of the exploration. The teacher continually added and deleted items as interest waned and additional learning opportunities presented themselves. Several other interests emerged as a result of the shadow activities. Batteries and flashlights were two notable hot topics.

Level 4

Essentially, Level 4 consists of centers based on independent, pair, or small-group activities. This level has the lowest amount of teacher control and highest level of student direction, as students design, supply, and operate the center. The teacher acts as facilitator and colearner and guides and assists the children in their learning activities. Dunn and Dunn (1972, 1992) and Renzulli and Reis (1997) have offered several useful management techniques for this type of center, one of which is the Contract Activity Packet (Dunn & Dunn, 1972). The contract is a written agreement between the student(s), the teacher(s), the parent(s), and anyone else involved in the center that details what the student will do, how the student will achieve the stated objective(s), and what everyone else involved will contribute.

This type of student-directed learning is often used in classrooms for gifted children, who typically have the ability, task commitment, persistence, and creativity to profit from naturalistic learning situations. Even young gifted children can engage in this type of learning when given appropriate background experience (with Levels 1, 2, and 3) and support and guidance.

In her first-grade classroom, one of the authors was addressing the Three R's—Recycle, Reuse, Repair. Having cycled through the preceding learning center levels, the children were ready to do Level 4 center activities. One group of five children planned a garden project, complete with a compost bin. One group of three studied cafeteria procedures, for example, weighing amounts of food thrown away. In the course of their contract projects, these two groups combined forces, and the cafeteria food waste was added to the garden compost bin. One child contacted local recycling centers and did a multimedia report on recycling procedures.

Conclusion

Learning centers have become a part of almost every early childhood classroom, including classrooms structured to meet the needs of young gifted children. As teachers become more sophisticated in the design and use of learning centers, children can benefit tremendously.

Each of the learning center levels is designed to meet both general and specific learning goals. Activities in the centers address goals and objectives in the developmental domains—cognitive, affective, and psychomotor—and also incorporate aspects of planning, self-direction, time management, the scientific method, and cooperative and independent learning. The learning centers are grounded in theory and practice, and they are closely tied to philosophy, curricular design, and methods of instruction. Although this chapter did not include a prescription for the use of the four levels, it did offer a general framework that can act as a guide for the teacher who wants to design and implement developmentally appropriate learning centers for young gifted children in the classroom.

References

Ausubel, D. P. (1963). *The psychology of meaningful verbal learning*. New York: Grune and Stratton.

Bloom, B. S. (1971). Mastery learning. In J. H. Block (Ed.) *Mastery learning: Theory and practice* (pp. 47–63). New York: Holt, Rinehart, & Winston.

Bruner, J. S. (1960). *The process of education*. New York: Vintage Books.

Bruner, J. S., Goodnow, J. J., & Austin, G. A. (1967). *A study of thinking*. New York: Science Editions.

Dewey, J. (1910). *How we think*. Boston: Heath.

Dewey, J. (1916). *Democracy in education*. New York: Macmillan.

Dunn, R., & Dunn, K. (1972). *Practical approaches to individualizing instruction: Contracts and other effective teaching strategies*. West Nyack, NY: Parker Publishing.

Dunn, R., & Dunn, K. (1992). *Teaching elementary students through their individual learning styles*. Boston: Allyn and Bacon.

Glasser, W. (1969). *Schools without failure*. New York: Harper & Row.

Good, T. L. (1983). Classroom research: A decade of progress. *Educational Psychologist, 18*, 127–144.

Gordon, W. J. J. (1961). *Synectics*. New York: Harper & Row.

Guskey, T. R., & Gates, S. L. (1986). Synthesis of research on the effects of mastery learning in elementary and secondary classrooms. *Educational Leadership, 43*(8), 73–80.

Johnson, D. W., Johnson, R. T., & Holubec, E. J. (1990). *Circles of learning: Cooperation in the classroom.* Edina, MN: Interaction Book Co.

Joyce, B., Weil, M., & Showers, B. (2003). *Models of teaching* (7th ed.). Boston: Allyn and Bacon.

Ornstein, A. C., & Hunkins, F. (1993). *Curriculum foundations, principles, and theory* (3rd ed.). Boston: Allyn and Bacon.

Renzulli, J. S., & Reis, S. M. (1997). *The schoolwide enrichment model: A how-to guide for educational excellence.* Mansfield Center, CT: Creative Learning Press.

Rogers, C. (1980). *A way of being.* Boston: Houghton Mifflin.

Rogers, C., & Freiberg, J. (1994). *Freedom to learn* (3rd ed.). Upper Saddle River, NJ: Prentice Hall.

Rosenshine, B. (1986). Synthesis of research on explicit teaching. *Educational Leadership, 43*(7), 60–69.

Slavin, R. (1994). *Cooperative learning: Theory, research, and practice* (2nd ed.). Boston: Allyn and Bacon.

Thelan, H. (1960). *Education and the human quest.* New York: Harper and Row.

chapter 11

Cooperative Learning
abused and overused?

by **Vickie Randall**

ducational fads come and go with predictable regularity. One such fad that has swept educational circles since the 1980s is known as cooperative learning. Cooperative learning has been touted as the panacea for "an astonishing array of educational problems" (Slavin, 1991, p. 71)—everything from alleviating the monotony of the traditional teacher-directed classroom, to the socialization of tomorrow's work force. So popular has cooperative learning become that its benefits may blind us to its drawbacks. In spite of its widespread acceptance, teachers and parents should be aware that cooperative learning exhibits three weaknesses.

One of these weaknesses is the basic premise upon which cooperative learning is based: Members of the group are responsible for each other's learning (Slavin, 1991). This is no doubt a heavy responsibility to place on young people. Even experienced teachers seldom wish to be held accountable for learning failures in their classrooms (try suggesting merit pay at the next faculty meeting). Yet, cooperative learning depends on this notion of responsibility: "the team's success depends on the individual learning of all team members" (Slavin, p. 73).

Therefore, in order to motivate members of the group to take each other's learning seriously, teachers are encouraged to employ one or more of the various models that have been proposed (Slavin, 1990a, 1991). For instance, team rewards may be offered to ensure that everyone finishes a worksheet or prepares for a quiz. The scores are totaled and rewards or grades are given based on team results. In another model, the scores of the group may be averaged, and the average score is assigned to each individual for a grade. A third proposal involves one score for a group project or assignment; this score becomes the grade for each person in the group.

This appears more than a trifle unfair. It would be handy if our democratic ideals could guarantee that students would learn equally or work equally, but they do not. We place too great a burden on children and teens not only by making them responsible for each other's learning (Can you ultimately be responsible for anyone's learning besides your own?), but also by grading them on how much other students learn. Acknowledging individual scores is a step in the right direction.

A second drawback to cooperative learning is the design of the cooperative learning group. It is typically composed of one high-achieving student, two of average ability, and one of low achievement (Johnson & Johnson, 1986; Slavin, 1991). In other words, the group is intentionally structured with students of mixed abilities, and for an obvious reason: If there is not at least one capable, articulate student in the group, who will "make sure that all team members have mastered the lesson" (Slavin, p. 73)?

Theoretically, those who fulfill this role of teacher in the cooperative learning group come to understand the material better as they explain it to the others. Nevertheless, some of these child-teachers complain about going over and over the same material they have already learned or having to explain it to those who could care less (Matthews, 1992). It is not only the bright students, however, who may suffer. One study (Mulryan, 1994) showed that, in groups of mixed ability, low-achieving students become passive and do not focus on the task, a difficulty I have seen repeatedly in elementary and junior high school groups. I have found even on the college level that, when

I assign group work, at least one person in the group will tend not to contribute, letting the others carry the load. In fact, cooperative learning presupposes that everyone in the group studies identical material (Slavin, Leavey, & Madden, 1984, p. 410), a formula for frustration.

Moreover, the idea that, in cooperative learning, "all students are learners and teachers" (Slavin, 1990a, p. 6) is probably unrealistic. William Chase (1989), as president of Wesleyan University, maintained that:

> The ways in which we cherish democracy and equality have allowed us to permit, sometimes encourage, the fictitious notion that a classroom of 24 students and one teacher actually holds 25 experts. After two decades of teaching experience, I want to assert that this is not so. (p. 124)

Thus, the design of the cooperative learning group is frequently self-defeating for at least some of the group members.

Cooperative learning, as it is often practiced, exhibits a third flaw, this one more subtle. In the words of one of cooperative learning's chief enthusiasts (Slavin, 1990b), "Cooperative learning is simply an instructional method, a means of effectively transmitting knowledge skills to students" (p. 29). Notice the choice of words: instructional method, transmitting, skills. These words illustrate the greatest shortcoming of cooperative learning: It lends itself to fact-based activities, to assignments that need to be "learned" or "mastered" (two words that appear repeatedly in the literature). The cooperative learning group therefore becomes another vehicle by which knowledge is acquired, rather than thinking encouraged.

Not that cooperative learning has to conform to this disposition; groups could engage in projects requiring higher order thinking, but that is usually not the case (Robinson, 1990; Ross, 1988). To put it simply, the cooperative learning group is an organizational device easily suited to routine skills and information transmission. Cooperative learning is, in fact, defined as a "classroom technique" (Slavin, 1980, p. 315), and a reliance on technique is not conducive to thoughtfulness. Accordingly, with its penchant for fact mastery, for neglecting rather than encouraging higher order thinking, cooperative learning as it is generally applied puts the very concept of real learning at risk.

The proponents of cooperative learning recommend that it be the dominant instructional strategy (Johnson & Johnson, 1986, p. 4), the primary instructional organization in the classroom (Slavin, Madden, & Stevens, 1990, as cited in Robinson, 1990, p. 19). Some teachers have told me that they do indeed use cooperative learning "all the time," "for everything." Should cooperative learning, or any other method for that matter, be the dominant strategy of any classroom? Can any procedural design be appropriate for everyone at all times?

Teachers could and probably should use cooperative learning on occasion, perhaps frequently devising their own configurations. For example, a group of gifted students could work together to see how far they could take a specific project. Or students from across the spectrum could be grouped so that those with complementary skills work together. Sometimes, those with similar talents, regardless of intellectual ability, might investigate areas of common interest. In addition, I have experienced success when students working on different activities come together temporarily to share what they have learned. It may be appropriate for a few students to visit other classrooms where they will find others who are on their level in a particular subject. It must be noted, however, that even with the many possible variations of cooperative learning, high-ability students often prefer to work alone.

Slavin (1990b) himself recommended that "districts need to first decide on their curricular goals, and only then look for instructional methods to achieve those goals" (p. 29). If our goals indicate that we value personal accountability, rewards commensurate with effort, and the cultivation of thought, we should consider very carefully before embracing cooperative learning inordinately. It does have a place in our classrooms; it can be beneficial under certain circumstances. But, to make cooperative learning our dominant instructional strategy is to ignore the weaknesses found in its basic premise, its design, and its propensity for fostering lower order thinking. It is not an all-purpose pill that will remedy every educational malady. The young people in our schools will be best served if cooperative learning is utilized judiciously. It should not be abused or overused.

References

Chase, W. (1989, March 27). Do universities and their students owe anything to the future? *The Commonwealth, 83*, 124–129.

Johnson, D., & Johnson, R. (1986*). Circles of learning: Cooperation in the classroom* (Rev. ed.). Edina, MN: Interaction Book.

Matthews, M. (1992). Gifted students talk about cooperative learning. *Educational Leadership, 50*(2), 48–50.

Mulryan, C. M. (1994). Perceptions of intermediate students' cooperative small-group work in mathematics. *Journal of Educational Research, 87*, 280–290.

Robinson, A. (1990). Cooperation or exploitation? The argument against cooperative learning for talented students. *Journal for the Education of the Gifted,14*, 9–27.

Ross, J. (1988). Improving social-environmental studies problem solving through cooperative learning. *American Educational Research Journal, 25*, 573–591.

Slavin, R. E. (1980). Cooperative learning. *Review of Educational Research, 50*, 315–342.

Slavin, R. E. (1990a). Ability grouping, cooperative learning, and the gifted. *Journal for the Education of the Gifted, 14*, 3–8.

Slavin, R. E. (1990b). Response to Robinson: Cooperative learning and the gifted: Who benefits? *Journal for the Education of the Gifted, 14*, 28–30.

Slavin, R. E. (1991). Synthesis of research on cooperative learning. *Educational Leadership, 48*(5), 71–82.

Slavin, R. E., Leavey, M., & Madden, N. (1984). Combining cooperative learning and individualized instruction: Effects on student mathematics achievement, attitudes, and behaviors. *Elementary School Journal, 84*, 409–422.

Slavin, R. E., Madden, N., & Stevens, R. (1990). Cooperative learning for the 3 R's. *Educational Leadership, 47*(4), 22–28.

Dealing With Under-achievement

chapter 12

Gifted Underachievement
oxymoron or educational enigma?

by **Barbara Hoover-Schultz**

ifted underachievement, at first glance, seems like an oxymoron. How can a gifted student also be an underachiever? By implicit definition gifted students are those who have developed high levels of intelligence and consistently perform at these high levels (Clark, 2002). Underachievement, on the other hand, is associated with a failure to do well in school. This seeming mismatch of terms is puzzling—giftedness and underachievement do not mesh. Like an oxymoron, they are at opposite ends of the educational spectrum. It is no wonder that the underachievement of gifted students is such a mystery.

Amazingly, estimates of students with high ability who do not achieve well are as high as 50% (Hoffman, Wasson, & Christianson, 1985; Rimm, 1987). This group represents a large population of talented students who are either underserved or neglected by gifted programs. If this many talented children are being ignored, it is imperative that the issue be addressed. However, a survey of the current literature demonstrates that educators disagree about the issue of gifted underachievement—not only in the definition, but the very legitimacy of gifted underachievement as a category of academic behavior. For example, Colangelo, Kerr, Christensen, and Maxey (2004) revealed that some researchers believe the majority of underachievement can simply be attributed to test error. Yet, psychologists, such as Sylvia Rimm, have spent their entire careers working to reverse underachievement.

A considerable number of articles, studies, and books have been written on the subject of gifted underachievement. Rather than clarifying a perplexing situation, the sheer amount of information and inconsistencies in definition muddies the waters. Without a clear definition, the concept of gifted underachievement remains elusive.

In an effort to understand and recognize gifted underachievement, this article will explore the definitions, characteristics, causes, and available interventions. Also, attention to underachievement in special populations will be briefly examined and discussed in an attempt to better understand this puzzling phenomenon.

Defining Underachievement in Gifted Students

Reis and McCoach (2000) pointed out that any discussion of the issue of gifted underachievement should begin with a definition. With all the assessments available to today's educators and the mountains of existing research, this should be a simple task. However, rather than one straightforward definition, many exist throughout the literature. Even more than two decades ago, Dowdall and Colangelo (1982) were already proposing that the concept of underachieving gifted students had become nearly meaningless due to numerous categories of definitions.

At first glance, gifted underachievers seem to have more in common with low achievers than high achievers, namely, low performance in the classroom. The interesting difference that sets the gifted underachiever apart from his or her counterpart, the low achiever, is the ability to score high on standardized achievement tests, which typically assess knowledge that is needed to perform well in the classroom. This discrepancy between ability and achievement is the basic ingredient that a majority of educators use in defining gifted underachievement.

Dowdall and Colangelo (1982) described three underlying themes in the definition of gifted underachievement:

1. Underachievement as a discrepancy between *potential* achievement and actual achievement.
2. Underachievement as a discrepancy between *predicted* achievement and actual achievement.
3. Underachievement as a failure to develop or use potential.

The most common definitions of gifted underachievement fall within the first theme; however, Reis and McCoach (2000) were quick to point out problems: the criteria used to identify giftedness varies from state to state and district to district, standardized tests may not directly reflect the actual school experience, and classroom grades may be unreliable and subjective.

Similar problems exist when attempting to define gifted underachievement using the second theme. No test is 100% reliable, especially when attempting to predict achievement. Something as simple as a bad mood or ill health on test day can skew achievement scores, resulting in measurement errors in prediction.

The third theme, underachievement as a failure to use potential, is more utilitarian in that it can be applied to all levels of learners. Rimm's (1997) definition of gifted underachievement fits this theme: "Underachievement is a discrepancy between a child's school performance and some index of the child's ability. If children are not working to their ability in school, they are underachieving" (p. 18). Even though Rimm was quick to point out that true underachievement problems are a matter of degree, her definition is a concise, easy-to-understand statement that explains the crux of gifted underachievement.

Once a working definition of gifted underachievement has been established, it is easier to explore its influences (or causes), as well as to describe common characteristics that set the stage for it. Like finding a definition, there is no one single event or factor that contributes to underachievement in gifted students. The causes of underachievement are complex (Fehrenbach,

1993), and a pattern that develops in elementary school often continues into the upper grades. There are a number of contributing factors to this pattern cited in the literature.

Gallagher (1991), Rimm (1997), and others have suggested that the causes of underachievement can be separated into environmental (school) factors and personal/family factors. Environmental factors appear to stem from two problem areas: the school and the student's peer group. An anti-intellectual school atmosphere that focuses on athletics and social status and an antigifted atmosphere can contribute to underachievement (Rimm, 1995). Inflexible requirements for graduation that require students to follow a specific path from entry to graduation may also contribute to low achievement in older gifted students. Underachieving students often report peer influence as the single most important force blocking their achievement (Reis & McCoach, 2000). A study that measured students' grades and behavior in the fall and spring found that students seemed to more closely resemble their friends at the end of the school year than at the beginning (Berndt, 1999), with their grades tending to decrease in the spring if their friends had lower grades in the fall. Is it any surprise that antiacademic peer groups could exert enough pressure on gifted students to cause them to hide their talents?

Underachievement related to personal matters often starts with unfavorable coping skills or learning styles. Research has attributed some difficulties encountered in these two areas to a form of neurological dysfunction or imbalance (Gallagher, 1991). However, the overwhelming factor appears to be in the area of personal/psychological underachievement due to dynamics within the family. Subsequent interactions at school add a layer of complication to an already perplexing situation. Interestingly, several characteristics of gifted underachievers were described decades ago by Lewis Terman in his famous longitudinal study of 1,500 gifted students. The underachieving group was set apart by the following characteristics (Gallagher):

- low levels of self-confidence;
- an inability to persevere;
- a lack of goals; and
- feelings of inferiority.

Contemporary researchers (Rimm, 1995; Whitmore, 1987) have confirmed Terman's findings that underachieving gifted students are different from achieving gifted students in personal and family relationships, as well as in self-image and motivation. Family is frequently identified as an unhealthy place for many gifted underachievers. Rimm and Lowe (1988) cited poor family relationships and inconsistent standards as being characteristic of the family dynamics of gifted underachievers: "commitment to career and respect for school were remarkably . . . absent" (p. 358). However, it may be that parents of underachieving students simply do not have the skills to support their children's unusual academic talents.

Culturally Diverse Underachievers

Gifted underachievement crosses all cultural boundaries and, interestingly, differs across the cultures. Pointing out that little research has focused specifically on culturally diverse underachievers, Reis and McCoach (2000) suggested that these students face unique barriers to achievement. For example, minority students are frequently underrepresented in gifted and talented programs, and different subcultures' definitions of achievement may differ from that of the dominant culture.

Language typically adversely affects gifted Latino students' achievement. Being proficient in English generally means greater success in school for Spanish-speaking students. However, it is not the only condition necessary for success. A different value system that exists within the Hispanic American community may be of greater impact, particularly for female students (Reis, 1998).

Identification practices may adversely affect gifted African American students. Baldwin (1987) suggested that the practices normally used to determine eligibility for gifted programs may not be valid or reliable for students from culturally diverse backgrounds; in particular, using intelligence scores as the sole criterion can create a bias toward African American students. Mickelson (1990) reported an attitude-achievement paradox: a positive attitude toward education coupled with low academic achievement that makes it difficult to reverse African American underachievement.

Gender differences also affect underachievement. According to a study done by Weiss (1972), approximately 25% of above-average females may be considered underachievers, as compared with approximately 50% of above-average males. Even though it appears that academically underachieving gifted girls are far outnumbered by underachieving gifted boys (Colangelo et al., 2004), increased attention has been aimed toward female under-achievers. Deliberate underachievement seems to be prevalent among bright adolescent females as a response to perceived sex-role expectations (Fox, 1981).

The issue of cultural diversity within the gifted population is beginning to receive more attention, particularly in the area of "hidden underachievers," students who underachieve because the educational system is not designed to recognize their talents. Because cultures vary in what is valued, should we impose one culture's ideas of achievement upon another's? Is this imposition helping children or, perhaps, hurting them? These questions need to be addressed before the underachievement of minority gifted students can be adequately addressed.

Interventions

Much has been written about the complex causes and characteristics of gifted underachievers, and the major points have been outlined above. However, understanding the causes and identification of gifted underachievers is only the first step. While appropriate interventions are necessary if educators are to correct this problem, it is understandable that proposed interventions have taken on several different directions. As with creating a definition and looking at causes of gifted underachievement, no single intervention has been found to be the answer. In fact, according to Reis and McCoach (2000), effective interventions designed to reverse underachievement in gifted students have been "inconsistent and inconclusive" (p. 202).

Butler-Por (1987), Dowdall and Colangelo (1982), and others have described two categories of interventions aimed at reversing gifted underachievement: counseling and instructional interventions. Counseling interventions attempt to change any personal or family dynamics affecting gifted students' under-achievement. Rather than attempting to force gifted students to be more successful, counseling interventions help them decide goals and help reverse any habits that are blocking the road to success. While some researchers believe the debate is still out on whether counseling interventions are truly successful, Rimm (1995) described a Trifocal Model used by schools with some success in reversing underachievement in gifted students. The six-step Trifocal Model begins with assessment and focuses on communication, changing expectations, identification, correc-tion of deficiencies, and modifications at home and school.

The second category of instructional interventions focuses on special classrooms designed to create a more favorable envi-ronment for gifted underachievers. These classrooms have a small teacher-student ratio and use less conventional approaches to teaching. Students typically have more freedom and control of their own learning. Unfortunately, this strategy has not encountered much success in reversing gifted underachieve-ment. Reasons for the lack of success range from educational politics, to difficulty in getting school districts to implement them due to limited time, physical space, and resources (Fehrenbach, 1993).

Why some programs work and others do not is almost as mysterious as the concept of gifted underachievement itself. However, Fine and Pitts (1980) devised some useful guidelines for planning and implementing successful intervention programs:

1. Initially develop a structure to support the child.
2. Issues, expectations, and intervention plans need to be solidly outlined.
3. Appoint one person to be in charge of the intervention plan.
4. Involve the family in a close, working relationship with the school.
5. Parents and teachers should establish a strong parental pos-ture to learning.
6. Group meetings should parallel family interactions.
7. Use follow-up conferences with the same people to main-tain accountability.
8. Expect and confront sabotages (pp. 53–54).

Successful intervention programs do not let the child be in charge. After all, underachieving children have shown their inability to work in their own best interest. However, through successful intervention over time, the child can be invited to be more active as problems and behavior issues are resolved.

Conclusions

As researchers (Dowdall & Colangelo, 1982; Fine & Pitts, 1980; Gallagher, 1991) have pointed out, gifted underachievers are more than smart children bored with school. There are far-reaching personal and political implications when gifted children—or any children, for that matter—do not work to their potential. The loss to society can be tragic.

An examination of the literature identifies general characteristics of gifted underachievers and suggests some causes for this peculiar phenomenon. The unique situation of culturally diverse gifted underachievers also requires attention. No panacea exists for resolving the issue of gifted underachievement, and unfortunately, it seems more questions arise than answers.

What can we do about the situation of gifted underachievement? Focusing on what we know, or at least what we think we know, as well as what we don't know, is a good place to start. We know that there are gifted students who are not performing to their potential and that there are a variety of causes and influences. However, educators do not have reliable information about how many gifted students are underachieving.

Intervention strategies exist with differing measures of success. Effective strategies are thought to reverse the problem of underachievement; unfortunately, such strategies, which include private programs, tend to be expensive and labor intensive. Is there a more efficient way to affect change?

Some researchers believe links between certain learning disabilities and gifted underachievement may suggest minor neurological problems. Is there something happening in our environment that produces this anomaly, or is it a genetic anomaly?

Out of questions answers may grow. Until that time, the process of defining underachievement, identifying underachieving gifted students, explaining underachievement, and suggesting interventions remains an educational enigma.

References

Baldwin, A. Y. (1987). I'm Black but look at me, I am also gifted. *Gifted Child Quarterly, 31*, 180–185.

Berndt, T. J. (1999). Friends' influence on students' adjustment to school. *Educational Psychologist, 34*, 15–28.

Butler-Por, N. (1987). *Underachievers in school.* New York: Wiley.

Clark, B. (2002). *Growing up gifted: Developing the potential of children at home and at school* (6th ed.). Upper Saddle River, NJ: Merrill/Prentice Hall.

Colangelo, N., Kerr, B., Christensen, P., & Maxey, J. (2004). A comparison of gifted underachievers and gifted high achievers. In S. M. Moon (Ed.). *Social/emotional issues, underachievement, and counseling of gifted and talented students* (pp. 119–132). Thousand Oaks, CA: Corwin Press.

Dowdall, C. B., & Colangelo, N. (1982). Underachieving gifted students: Review and implications. *Gifted Child Quarterly, 26*, 179–184.

Fehrenbach, C. R. (1993). Underachieving gifted students: Intervention programs that work. *Roeper Review, 16*, 88–90.

Fine, M. J., & Pitts, R. (1980). Intervention with underachieving gifted children: Rationale and strategies. *Gifted Child Quarterly, 24*, 51–55.

Fox, L. H. (1981). Preparing gifted girls for future leadership roles. *Gifted, Creative, & Talented, 17*, 7–11.

Gallagher, J. J. (1991). Personal patterns of underachievement. *Journal for the Education of the Gifted, 14*, 221–233.

Hoffman, J. L., Wasson, F. R., & Christianson, B. P. (1985). Personal development for the gifted underachiever. *Gifted Child Today, 8*(3), 12–14.

Mickelson, R. A. (1990). The attitude achievement paradox among Black adolescents. *Sociology of Education, 63*, 44–61.

Reis, S. M. (1998). Underachievement for some—dropping out with dignity for others. *Communicator, 29*(1), 19–24.

Reis, S. M., & McCoach, D. B. (2000). The underachievement of gifted students: What do we know and where do we go? *Gifted Child Quarterly, 44*, 152–170.

Rimm, S. (1987). Creative underachievers: Marching to the beat of a different drummer. *Gifted Child Today, 10*(1), 2–6.

Rimm, S. B. (1995). *Why bright kids get poor grades and what you can do about it.* New York: Three Rivers Press.

Rimm, S. B. (1997). An underachievement epidemic. *Educational Leadership, 54*(7), 18–22.

Rimm, S., & Lowe, B. (1988). Family environments of underachieving gifted students. *Gifted Child Quarterly, 32*, 353–361.

Weiss, L. (1972). Underachievement—empirical studies. *Journal of Adolescence, 3*, 143–151.

Whitmore, J. (1987). Conceptualizing the issue of underserved populations of gifted students. *Journal for the Education of the Gifted, 10*, 141–154.

chapter 13

Motivating the Gifted Underachiever

implementing reward menus and behavioral contracts within an integrated approach

by **Earl S. Hishinuma**

*t*he Scene: End-of-the-Year Parent Conference

Teacher: Thank you Mr. and Mrs. Jones for coming to the last parent conference of the school year. Please have a seat. I'm glad that John could also make it to this conference.

Let me start by saying that this school year was a struggle for John. As you can see from his report card, he earned two F grades, one in spelling, and one in writing. John's C and D grades were in reading, math, art, social studies, and P.E. He received just one A, and that was in science. We all know that John can do better; he just isn't reaching his full potential. I'm sure you've heard that before. John really needs to put in more effort; he's just not motivated except maybe in science when doing laboratory work like dissecting sharks and mixing chemicals. Oh, and I also have his standardized achievement test results, which were administered about a month ago. As you can see, all of his scores are well above average. In fact, he is excelling in most of his subjects.

Parents: Why is it that John does so well on standardized tests and sometimes on classroom quizzes, but is just not able to earn higher course grades? We're getting tired of this year after year.

Teacher: His grades are impacted by his lack of attention during class, incomplete class assignments, late completion of homework, and overall low standards for the quality of his own work. John knows this; we've talked many times before. A lot of this is really up to John. He should be getting A's and B's in all of his subjects. I hope John takes more responsibility for his learning in the future.

Parents: We know how you feel. We've been hearing the same old story ever since John entered kindergarten. Some teachers have called John unmotivated, irresponsible, and even lazy. But, what we don't understand is that he can play video games at home for hours on end, and he will go through his baseball card collection and memorize the most irrelevant statistics. And he loves to solve brain teasers and play games that involve a lot of thinking. So, what's going on? What can the school, and what can we, as parents, do for him?

Teacher: Well, let's ask John.

John is fidgeting with his digital watch, wishing that time would go by much faster. The nearest parent gets John's attention by tapping him on the arm.

Teacher: John, why don't you put in more effort? How can we help?

John shrugs his shoulders to say, "I don't know." Then, he immediately resumes playing with his watch.

What Can Be Done?

The essence of this interchange should be familiar to most teachers (see Cohen, 1990). Although the gifted/underachiever population is as diverse as any other group of individuals, the common theme is the student not meeting his or her potential as reflected by an academic measure of performance (e.g., class-work, grades, homework production, quizzes, tests). This lack of productivity is not due to an inherent disability such as a learning disability or behavior disorder. Characteristics of the gifted underachiever may include high IQ and problem-solving abilities, avoidance of rote and repetitive tasks, inconsistent completion of academic work, good oral performances rather than written products, variable test results, restricted or nontraditional interests, low self-esteem, low or too high self-standards, self-centeredness, difficulty functioning constructively in a group, unresponsiveness to typical social rewards such as praise and grades, and school-attendance problems (see Whitmore, 1980).

According to Cohen (1990), "Though more underachievers pervade the school system than all of the special education students combined, there are virtually no special services available to help them" (p. 3). This lack of programs for underachievers is at least partially due to our society's tendency to label the underachiever as being unresponsive and even lazy. These everyday "diagnoses" tend to thrust upon the student virtually full responsibility for "getting his or her act together," rather than examining more closely the home and school environments to see if adjustments in the student's settings will result in positive changes in his or her behavior. In short, because there is no society-accepted "disability," the "problem" falls squarely on the student's shoulders.

The view taken in this chapter is that (a) the difficulties associated with underachievement and gifted underachievement should be addressed from an integrated-systems approach given the multifaceted issues involved, and (b) specific interventions, particularly reward menus and behavioral contracts, can be developed and implemented successfully with the goal of meeting the needs of these students.

An Integrated Approach

From the fields of education and psychology, growing attention in the past few decades has been paid to the underachiever and gifted underachiever (e.g., Butler-Por, 1987; Cohen, 1990; Griffin, 1988; Kornrich, 1965; Mandel & Marcus, 1988; Rimm, 1986; Supplee, 1990; Whitmore, 1980). A recurring central theme is that the gifted underachiever cannot be viewed in isolation from home, school, and social settings. The following factors all need to be considered in developing a well-rounded and appropriate plan of action for the gifted underachiever:

- comprehensive and ongoing assessment;
- teacher attributes;
- curricula and instruction;
- social/emotional development and counseling;
- school philosophy and procedures; and
- parenting and the home environment.

Comprehensive and Ongoing Assessment

In most cases, the underachiever is noticed by the teacher because he or she is not performing up to teacher expectations for the class. However, for the gifted underachiever, underidentification may be more prevalent because the giftedness may be masked by grade-level performance (e.g., Hishinuma, 1990; Whitmore, 1980). In addition, the possibility of a learning disability or behavior disorder must be ruled out in an effort to develop an appropriate program for the student.

For these reasons, referral for comprehensive testing may be a prudent choice. More subtle academic and social/emotional strengths and weaknesses should be ascertained on a daily basis, as well. For example, does the gifted underachiever have the prerequisite skills necessary to perform a given task? Are the teacher-determined assignments too easy or too difficult for the student? Further assessments should be done throughout the school year to monitor the student's progress, with adjustments incorporated as needed.

Teacher Attributes

The attributes of the teacher are important factors in the success of the gifted underachiever. The teacher is the professional who will have the most firsthand, daily social contact with the student in the school setting. The programs developed and implemented by the teacher should make an impact on the student on academic and social/emotional levels. The teacher should be realistic about what he or she can accomplish in the classroom and school environment, but should also be as innovative as possible in the techniques utilized to improve the services provided to the gifted underachiever.

Curricula and Instruction

A critical component to a successful comprehensive program for the gifted underachiever is devising and implementing appropriate curricula and instruction. In general, most experts recommend that the teaching methods consist of hands-on, applied, and exciting activities that tap the strengths (i.e., higher level thinking skills) of the gifted underachiever (Supplee, 1990). Instructional formats can be greatly enhanced through strategic diversification: increased student-teacher feedback (see Heward, Gardner, Cavanaugh, Courson, Grossi, & Barbetta, 1995, for an example of using response cards), group and class discussions, games, videos, plays, computer projects, enrichment activities, student/teacher-agreed-upon independent projects, academic-interest centers, and field trips (Supplee). The benefits of a more varied curricular approach are not only increased learning, retention, and application skills, but also added motivation for the student to perform well. In most situations, the teacher wants to take full advantage of the motivating properties of his or her diverse, hands-on, applied, and interesting teaching methods. Such techniques will decrease the need for more externally based and artificial means of enhancing student performance.

Social/Emotional Development and Counseling

In attempting to increase the motivational level of the gifted underachiever, a more incremental intervention approach—ranging from fostering awareness, to providing tangible rewards—may be useful. For example, an elaborate behavioral contract system may not be necessary, as the student may alter his or her behavior due to the following gradient of interventions: Make the student aware of the natural consequences of his or her behavior, implement an informal self-monitoring and self-reinforcement system, or formalize the self-monitoring system and link improvements to specific rewards. It is best to utilize the least obtrusive means of altering behavior.

Intricately tied to motivated performance is the social/emotional development of the gifted underachiever. Issues of self-concept, coping skills, and peer relations can indirectly or directly impact the student's productivity both in and outside of the school setting. Benefit may be found in not neglecting the oftentimes simple, but effective methods of counseling for the gifted underachiever (Hishinuma, 1993; Yoshimoto & Lundell, 1992). For instance, lack of homework timeliness and quality may be due to an unstructured home environment, rather than poor study skills. Interventions may be more effective if family-related concerns are addressed first. In addition, counseling the student in the school environment might enhance self-concept (Canfield & Siccone, 1993; Canfield & Wells, 1976; Siccone & Canfield, 1993), teach coping skills (e.g., how to cope with a boring lecture), and improve social skills (e.g., how to deal with being teased, how to interact with students with different interests). The availability of a school counselor will also influence the interventions taken.

Additional attention may be necessary for more persistent or severe difficulties in behavior and social/emotional development. Table 13.1 delineates behavioral characteristics associated with disorders that may be encountered by the teacher. If significant behaviors are suspected, an appropriate school official should be consulted and a comprehensive evaluation should be considered (if not already conducted). If confirmed by a qualified professional or multidisciplinary team, appropriate services outside the school setting (e.g., medications, psychotherapy, etc.) may be necessary to complement in-school programs.

Table 13.1. Behavioral Characteristics for Possible Referral for Comprehensive Testing and/or Mental Health Evaluation

ADHD—Predominantly inattentive type	careless errors, distractibility, lack of sustained attention, poor listening skills, difficulty following through, poor organization, avoidance of difficult tasks, loss of things, forgetfulness
ADHD—Predominantly hyperactive-impulsive type	Hyperactive—restlessness, difficulty remaining in seat, physically active, difficulty playing quietly, "on the go," excessively talks. Impulsive—blurted out answers, difficulty awaiting turn, interruption of others
Anxiety-Related	restlessness, ease in being fatigued, difficulty concentrating, ease in being irritable, muscle tension, sleep disturbance
Conduct Disorder	aggressive, property destruction, deceitfulness, theft, serious violation of rules
Oppositional Defiant Disorder	temper loss, argument, defiance/refusal of adult requests, deliberate annoyance of others, ease in being annoyed, external blame, anger/resentfulness, spitefulness/vindication
Depression	interest/pleasure loss, change in eating habits and weight loss or gain, change in sleeping patterns, energy loss, feelings of worthlessness, diminished ability to think/concentrate, suicidal ideation

Note. Adapted from American Psychiatric Association (1994).

School Philosophy and Procedures

The school's philosophy and resulting procedures may impact the services developed and implemented by the teacher in his or her classroom. School policies and procedures that provide consistency across classrooms and courses allow for a predictable environment for the gifted underachiever. For example, consistency in classroom management and homework policies across the school aids the student in adjusting to the school's expectations. In contrast, inconsistencies in schoolwide policies make the situation more difficult for the gifted underachiever because he or she must keep track of and adjust to the different and idiosyncratic rules for each teacher, classroom, and course. For instance, if one teacher attempts to motivate the student to complete homework assignments by contacting the student's parents and another teacher tries to handle all homework issues within the parameters of the school, then one could expect the student to be somewhat confused. In the end, one system may be more effective than the other, but the two systems may also work against each other in the long run. In general, this type of inconsistency in homework policy will be to the detriment of the gifted underachiever.

Ideally, the schoolwide philosophy and procedures should be supportive of the gifted underachiever. For example, teacher in-services could focus on such topics as informal assessments, curriculum development, instructional game formats, computer and technological applications, motivational techniques, and counseling methods related to the gifted underachiever.

Parenting and the Home Environment

Although the emphasis of this chapter is on what can be done in the school setting, factors associated with the home and family will affect the characteristics of the gifted underachiever and what interventions may be effective in the classroom. For instance, if a behavioral contract is entered between a teacher and student, but the ultimate reward is already being provided in the home environment, then the outcome will almost assuredly be disappointing. Therefore, at a minimum, parent-school communication, collaboration, and mutual support are essential components to motivating the gifted underachiever successfully.

Reward Menus and Behavioral Contracts

Reward menus and behavioral contracts have been used in many different types of environments, including schools, in an effort to increase the motivational level and performance of individuals. Seven general steps are needed to develop and implement a behavioral approach that enhances gifted underachiever motivation.

Step 1: Target Behaviors

The first procedure in this seven-step process is identifying and targeting the behaviors in question. Different aspects of a behavior can be addressed: frequency, duration, and intensity. In addition, it is important to note that, in targeting undesirable behaviors (e.g., daydreaming in class), there should be equal emphasis on selecting desirable behaviors, as well (e.g., attending). The combination of rewarding productive, desirable behaviors while attempting to eliminate undesirable behaviors is the most effective method. Positive behaviors to target may include being on time to class, being prepared for class with all necessary materials, turning in homework assignments on time, turning in homework of quality, working on class assignments without teacher prompting, making eye contact with the teacher, taking notes, working independently, participating in class discussions, and recording homework assignments. Undesirable behaviors may include being tardy to class, attending to events outside of the classroom, talking and distracting peers, doodling instead of taking notes, and rushing out of the classroom without recording the homework assignment.

Step 2: Obtain Baselines

When formal research is conducted, quantification of the targeted behaviors is important to determine if progress is being made by the student. Although such standardized observational procedures are helpful in conveying an accurate picture of the student's behavior, the teacher may not have the resources to collect behavioral data on such a precise level. However, the teacher should obtain some sense of a "baseline" of the behaviors in order to evaluate the effectiveness of the behavioral program. This baseline could be as simple as knowing that the student comes in late to class 4 out of 5 days or turns in his or her homework only about once every 5 days.

Step 3: Determine Positive Rewards and Consequences

The third step is to determine the possible rewards and, if necessary, the mild negative consequences that may be used to increase motivation. One flexible and effective means of fulfilling this step is to construct a reward menu (or reinforcer menu) for each student in need of a more structured approach, or perhaps for the entire class (Alberto & Troutman, 1990; McCartney, 1989). A reward menu consists of a list of reinforcers from which the student may select based on an agreed-upon point system. The contents of the reward menu may be determined using two complementary methods: (a) have the student respond to open-ended questions, and (b) have the student select from an already made-up reward menu of potential reinforcers.

The following questions may be posed to the gifted underachiever in an open-ended format:

Tangible Rewards
- What kinds of things or items in school and at home do you like? This can include things to eat or drink, school supplies, toys, games, and so on.
- If someone gave you $1, what would you buy?
- If someone gave you $10, what would you buy?

Social Rewards
- Who are your best friends?
- What kinds of things do you like to do with your classmates?
- What kinds of ways do you like others to know that you did something positive?

Activity Rewards
- What kinds of activities do you like to do in the classroom?

- What kinds of activities do you like to do outside of the classroom? What kinds of activities do you like to do at home?
- Do you have any hobbies? If so, what are they?

Table 13.2 is an already prepared sample reward menu that can be modified based on the student, teacher, and school in question. The items and activities listed can be a starting point for the gifted underachiever.

Individualization. The reward menu will have greater effectiveness if the contents are determined by the student and subsequently approved or disapproved by the teacher. For example, having more recess time is a positive reward for most students. However, for many students who lack social skills, interacting with their peers during recess may actually be an aversive event. Similarly, collecting insects may be extremely motivating for one gifted underachiever, but may be quite repulsive for another. Therefore, although empirically based ratings of reinforcer strength should be considered (e.g., Fantuzzo, Rohrbeck, Hightower, & Work, 1991), the teacher must focus in on what is reinforcing for each particular gifted underachiever.

Class Menu. The concept of a reward menu can be extended to the entire class, so that the class as a whole can select rewards based on class achievements. However, the teacher should be careful in applying what will amount to "group contingencies." If not done with a distinct strategy in mind, such a program can instigate difficulties in peer relations when class goals are not met due to any one particular student or small group of students. In addition, group contingencies that allow for only one mischievous student to "wreck" the rewards of the entire class may give undue attention and control to this one student. Therefore, structuring for success for the entire class is a prudent strategy along with taking into account students who may have difficulty contributing to a group contingency.

Resistance to Deprivation-Satiation Effects. One distinct advantage of using a reward menu is that the wide selection of reinforcers greatly decreases the chances of the student becom-

Table 13.2. **Possible Individual and Class Reward Menu**

Tangible Rewards
- food (candy, raisin, fruit, popcorn, cookies, chips, crackers, juice, milk, soda)
- school stationery (pencils, pens, erasers, notepads, stamps, and pads)
- "little" things (stickers, toys, Frisbees, balls)
- high-interest items (magazines, comics, books, magnets, CDs)
- larger items supported by parents (calculators, inline skates, videogames)
- money-based rewards (e.g.,work study, allowance)

Social Rewards
- social praise from class, teacher, school counselor, principal
- display of work on bulletin board, hallway
- grades, awards, certificates
- study time with friends
- choice of where to sit in class
- free time to socialize
- group discussions and decisions
- group leader
- "auction" conductor
- peer tutor/teacher, peer counselor
- "special" time with teacher, counselor, principal
- "assistant" or expert for the teacher (e.g. teacher's assistant, computer assistant)
- positive note home to parents

Activity Rewards
Academic, Educational
- read, tell/listen to stories
- make or play games, solve puzzles
- engage in hands-on activities such as LEGO Logo, models
- rockets,jewelry making
- conduct science experiments (e.g., dissection, microscope)
- use of computer, video equipment
- utilize "centers" of interest
- select and watch videos
- go to the library, go on field trips
- design an area of the class
- earn "passes" for homework and tests

Arts
- draw, color, paint; make clay pieces, craft items; listen to music; plan a humorous skit

Physical Sports
- more recess time, swings, tag, kickball, dodgeball

Celebrations
- have a party, be excused early

ing tired of all of the rewards at the same time. For example, tangible reinforcers such as food and drinks are generally rewarding only to the extent that the student has been deprived of these items. Once the pupil is satiated or "full" (e.g., after lunch), food may no longer be an effective reinforcer. With the inclusion of social and activity-based rewards, the probability becomes low that the student will become tired of all of the reinforcers on the reward menu.

Step 4: Set Realistic Goals When Linking Behavior to Rewards and Consequences

The fourth step is to solidify a realistic point system linking the behavioral goals to rewards and consequences. Each behavioral goal should be worth a certain number of points. Likewise, each item on the reward menu should be assigned a certain number of points in order to be "bought" or attained. Although the student should provide input in the process, the teacher should have the last say. This step is one of open discussion, but the process should not turn into a negotiation in which the student and teacher are equals. The teacher is in control, but willing to listen to the student's suggestions. Successfully completing this step can be a delicate matter. If the point assignments are too liberal, the student may earn so many of the items on the reward menu that he or she may not "put out" as much as desired. If the point system is too stringent, the student may not attain enough success and may not respond constructively to the program.

However, at the beginning, there are advantages to setting up behavioral goals that are almost guaranteed to be met, thus resulting in the gifted underachiever being rewarded and feeling successful. This structuring of success should increase motivation to attain higher goals in the future. For example, one goal might be to improve homework timeliness by going from turning in only one assignment on time in a given week to two or three. Although such a goal may seem trivial in light of the ultimate objective of, say, 90 or 100%, the expectation on the student's part is to improve twofold or threefold in a week's time frame, which is considerable.

In addition, in an effort to structure for success, behaviors may need to be broken down into more manageable units. For example, instead of targeting the global and complex behavior of completion of a term paper, the teacher may consider breaking down the term paper task into more manageable behaviors: Have the student determine the topic, collect five resources, take notes for each resource, organize the notes, complete the introduction, write the first half of the body, finish the second half of the body, complete the conclusion, produce the bibliography, proof and double-check the draft, and complete and turn in the final version. Each of these more specific behaviors could be made into a goal and rewards could be provided accordingly. Part of the difficulty for the gifted underachiever is that the rewards of completing a term paper are traditionally provided on a very delayed basis in comparison to the initial behaviors.

As can be deduced, the point system offers great flexibility. Another advantage is that implementation of the program can be done with minimal disruption to instruction. In fact, elaborate classroom systems can be developed, including those that incorporate math, consumerism, economics, and banking (e.g., Adair & Schneider, 1993). For example, each student could have a savings or checking account. Deposit slips and checks could be mass-produced with scratch paper. Interest from the accounts could be calculated. The stock market could be integrated into the activities by allowing students to buy and sell stocks. A class or school "store" could be created as a central location for many of the rewards. Periodic "auctions" could be held for the highly desirable, one-of-a-kind rewards (some donated by parents). Students could volunteer for various "occupations" such as bank teller, store cashier, stock broker, and auctioneer. And woven throughout this economic organizational structure could be the point system.

Although taking away points, a form of punishment called "response cost," would be one additional way to increase flexibility in the system and enhance student motivation, a more positive approach is suggested at first. This positive orientation, along with ignoring undesirable behavior or applying very mild forms of punishment (e.g., time out), may be sufficient to change behavior to a desirable level. In addition, natural consequences should be utilized to a greater extent than artificial consequences because the message to the student will be less vindictive and will likely foster generalization of behavior to other environments where actual natural consequences also exist.

Step 5: Determine Means of Recordkeeping, Feedback, and Cashing In

When agreements are reached on the points assigned to behavioral goals and rewards, a behavioral contract is formed. As part of the behavioral contract, the method of recordkeeping, providing feedback to the student, and "cashing in" points and obtaining rewards should be solidified.

Recordkeeping. The teacher should select the most effective, accurate, and least cumbersome method for recordkeeping. Stars, check marks, tallies, and numbered points can be utilized to keep track of the points earned. The records can be kept on an index card on the student's desk, in a specific folder on the teacher's desk, or, if done in a positive manner, on the class bulletin board. Whenever possible, the student should be allowed to assist in the recordkeeping process, with the teacher being able to verify the information as needed. When a classwide point system is implemented, perhaps the last 5 to 10 minutes per day can be utilized for recordkeeping. This will be time well spent given the benefits of improved student performance.

Feedback to the Student. Feedback to the student on how many points earned is an important component to a successful program. In general, the more immediate this feedback is to the gifted underachiever, the more effective the behavioral program will be. One way to maintain immediate feedback, but not burden the teacher with this sometimes laborious task, is to have the student become more involved in the recordkeeping. However, the recordkeeping and feedback should not interfere with the student's performance in the classroom setting.

Cashing In. The method of cashing in points should be diverse and flexible, but not to the point of interrupting instructional time. For example, the teacher may set the following time frames for cashing in: just before the start of the school day, after the completion of in-class assignments, in between class periods, during the first 5 minutes of lunch, and immediately after school. For a classwide system, a short amount of time could be devoted daily or weekly to access the class store or conduct a classwide auction.

Finally, to decrease any misunderstanding concerning the intricacies of the behavioral contract, the student should be asked to paraphrase back to the teacher the exact details of the agreement. Although such a contract can remain on an oral level, jotting down the main components is a good idea just in case future reference is needed. As part of any contract, the student should clearly understand that the teacher has the right to modify it at any time, although when this is done, the teacher should explain the reasons to the student, rather than invoking a seemingly arbitrary rule. Ideally, the contract can be printed out and signed by all parties involved, including the student, teacher, and, where appropriate, school counselor, principal, and parents (DeRisi & Butz, 1975).

Step 6: Implement and Modify the Program

When implementing the program, it should be emphasized that the teacher is monitoring the student's behavioral progress, evaluating the effectiveness of the program, and continually considering changes to the system. Very few programs can be spelled out in detail from the start and result in the desired outcomes without any modifications to the system.

However, if the gifted underachiever has been structured for success from the start, he or she should attain most of his or her behavioral goals early on. Positive rewards should be accompanied by social acknowledgments, as well (e.g., "You really did a nice job!"). Aside from minor reminders of the conditions of the contract, no warnings, threats, or intimidating statements should be made to the student. The agreements have already been determined, and in the process of paraphrasing, the student has already confirmed to the teacher his or her understanding of the terms. Any type of negative consequences should be implemented in a matter-of-fact manner with minimal embarrassment to the student.

In the course of executing the program, loopholes should be closed, and as the student's behavior improves, expectations should be increased in reasonable increments. However, the teacher should expect "two steps forward, one step back," given the complexity of human behavior.

Step 7: Increase Maintenance, Generalization, and Intrinsic Motivation

When considering whether or not to develop a behavioral program, the ultimate goal for most students, gifted underachievers included, should be to eventually wean them off of such a structured system, especially if tangible rewards are a large part of the reward menu. However, such a weaning process should be done systematically and strategically. Behavioral expectations should be gradually increased in response to successful attainment of previous goals. Rewards should be provided on a more intermittent and delayed basis. For example, if the initial behavioral goal was for the student to earn one point by remaining on task for 10 minutes, the next modified goal might be for the student to earn two points by remaining on task for 20 minutes. If the student is successful in both cases, the same amount of reward is actually earned. However, the greater expectation is in the duration of on-task behaviors. In addition, the student should be guided increasingly toward social and activity-based rewards. Self-monitoring and self-reinforcement methods should be incorporated.

Conclusion

The teacher is up against a formidable task. Typically, the gifted underachiever has displayed a lifelong pattern of "not meeting his or her potential." The teacher is tasked with turning this student around (along with meeting the needs of 25 or 30 other students); but, realistically, he or she has access to a restricted range of reinforcers that may or may not be potent and effective enough to change the student's behavior. For example, in contrast to the rewards available in the school setting, the gifted underachiever may have access to the following at home: inline skates, bicycle, private bedroom equipped with a TV set for watching shows and playing videogames, Internet access, portable videogames, CD player, and telephone. In the school environment, the teacher may be offering rewards such as stickers, rubber stamps, and 5 minutes of computer time. The discrepancy in the availability of reinforcers between the home and school must be factored in when setting behavioral goals.

While this set of circumstances can be discouraging to the teacher, he or she should be fully cognizant that the school environment also offers reinforcers that are less likely to occur in the home, including social and activity-based rewards. Taking full advantage of these is a key to motivating the gifted underachiever. The additional advantage of using social and activity-based reinforcers is that these rewards are usually intrinsically based to begin with, which increases the likelihood of maintenance and generalization to other environments.

More fundamentally, a common criticism of using rewards, especially external or tangible ones, is that we are essentially bribing the student. Because this is a frequent concern and will often lead parents and teachers to not consider using the techniques proposed in this chapter, the issue is addressed here (see also Axelrod, 1983).

First, the present view is not to utilize tangible rewards if the student in question is self-directed and intrinsically motivated. In general, do not "fix" something that is not broken. However, for the gifted underachiever who has been counseled and provided appropriate services, but is still not responsive to the school's programs, a more structured behavioral approach may be warranted. In this regard, two relevant definitions of *bribe* are provided by *Webster's New Universal Unabridged Dictionary* (1983). The first states, "a price, reward, gift, or favor bestowed or promised to induce one to commit a wrong or illegal act" (p. 226). For instance, if someone pays a government official to do something illegal, then this would fall under the first definition of bribe. Clearly, the reward provided to a student for being on task or for turning in homework on time cannot be considered a bribe because the behaviors in question are neither wrong nor illegal, and in fact, are productive and prosocial in nature. The second definition of bribe is as follows: "anything given or promised to induce a person to do something against his wishes" (p. 226). This definition is what concerns most people and makes them philosophically against providing rewards for expected behaviors. Many parents feel that they should not have to bribe and pay their children to behave appropriately (e.g., children should keep their rooms neat and clean for their own sake). Likewise, teachers may feel that they should not bribe or give rewards such as toys for students being on task or for homework production. Although this definition of bribe technically applies in these cases, adults may be providing students with a double standard. In particular, most adults would not work without pay; yet, we expect students to attend school and perform at a high level for a minimum of 13 straight years (i.e., kindergarten through the 12th grade) without so much as a penny.

For some groups of students like gifted underachievers, such an arrangement is a set-up for failure. The typical rewards provided by teachers and schools may not be potent enough or provided on an immediate enough basis to maintain the effortful behaviors that are required. If we wish to be effective with gifted underachievers, we must at times recognize how ineffective the environment is for such students. Giving 100% of the responsibility to the student and waiting for more natural consequences to "kick in" (e.g., not being accepted into college, not being able to get a job, etc.) may be high prices to pay that are out of proportion to the relatively manageable programs that can be developed and implemented in the earlier years of schooling.

Determining how to motivate gifted underachievers can be a frustrating process if there appears to be no effective alternative. Many teachers have not had the necessary training to tackle such a formidable task. The usual methods such as teacher praise and grades may not suffice for the gifted underachiever. Therefore, this chapter has suggested a multifaceted and integrated approach to increasing motivation in gifted underachievers.

References

Adair, J. G., & Schneider, J. L. (1993). Banking on learning: An incentive system for adolescents in the resource room. *Teaching Exceptional Children, 25*(2), 30–35.

Alberto, P. A., & Troutman, A. C. (1990). *Applied behavior analysis for teachers* (3rd ed.). Columbus, OH: Merrill.

American Psychiatric Association (APA). (1994). *Diagnostic and statistical manual of mental disorders* (4th ed.). Washington, DC: Author.

Axelrod, S. (1983). *Behavior modification for the classroom teacher* (2nd ed.). New York: McGraw-Hill.

Butler-Por, N. (1987). *Underachievers in school: Issues and intervention.* New York: Wiley.

Canfield, J., & Siccone, F. (1993). *101 ways to develop student self-esteem and responsibility. Vol I: The teacher as coach.* Boston: Allyn and Bacon.

Canfield, J., & Wells, H. C. (1976). *100 ways to enhance self-concept in the classroom: A handbook for teachers and parents.* Englewood Cliffs, NJ: Prentice Hall.

Cohen, V. C. (1990). *Boosting the underachiever: How busy parents can unlock their child's potential.* New York: Plenum Press.

DeRisi, W. J., & Butz, G. (1975). *Writing behavioral contracts: A case simulation practice manual.* Champaign, IL: Research Press.

Fantuzzo, J. W., Rohrbeck, C. A., Hightower, A. D., & Work, W. C. (1991). Teachers' use and children's preferences of rewards in elementary school. *Psychology in the Schools, 28*, 175–181.

Griffin, R. S. (1988). *Underachievers in secondary schools: Education off the mark.* Hillsdale, NJ: Erlbaum.

Heward, W. L., Gardner III, R., Cavanaugh, R. A., Courson, F. H., Grossi, T. A., & Barbetta, P. M. (1995). Everyone participates in this class: Using response cards to increase active student response. *Teaching Exceptional Children, 28*(2), 4–11.

Hishinuma, E. S. (1990). *A theoretical and pragmatic application of paradigmatic behaviorism: Screening and identification of high potential/underachievers currently in regular education.* Ann Arbor, MI: University Microfilms International. (Order #9030561)

Hishinuma, E. S. (1993). Counseling gifted/at risk and gifted/dyslexic youngsters. *Gifted Child Today, 16*(1), 30–33.

Kornrich, M. (Ed.). (1965). *Underachievement.* Springfield, IL: Thomas.

Mandel, H. P., & Marcus, S. I. (1988). *The psychology of underachievement: Differential diagnosis and differential treatment.* New York: Wiley.

McCartney, S. B. (1989). *The attention deficit disorders intervention manual.* Columbia, MO: Hawthorne Educational Services.

Rimm, S. B. (1986). *Underachievement syndrome: Causes and cures.* Watertown, WI: Apple.

Siccone, F., & Canfield, J. (1993). *101 ways to develop student self-esteem and responsibility. Vol II: The power to succeed in school and beyond.* Boston: Allyn and Bacon.

Supplee, P. L. (1990). *Reaching the gifted underachiever: Program strategy and design.* New York: Teachers College Press.

Whitmore, J. R. (1980). *Giftedness, conflict, and underachievement.* Boston: Allyn and Bacon.

Yoshimoto, R., & Lundell, F. (1992, May). *Integration of counseling modalities.* Paper presented at the annual meeting of the Association for the Education of Gifted Underachieving Students, New Rochelle, NY.

chapter 14

Setting "Motivation Traps" for Underachieving Gifted Students

by Donna Y. Ford, Sheila R. Alber, *and* William L. Heward

"There are three important things to remember about education. The first one is motivation, the second is motivation, and the third is motivation."

—Terrell Bell
(former Secretary,
U.S. Department of Education)

Student motivation, or rather its absence, is a troubling and persistent problem in education. In most classrooms, teachers voice frustration and concerns about poor student motivation—disinterest, lack of engagement, off-task behaviors—and its impact on student achievement. According to Newmann (1992), "the most pressing and persistent issue for students and teachers is not low achievement, but student engagement. Students attend class but with little excitement, commitment, and pride in mastering the curriculum. They have no psychological investment in learning" (p. 2).

Poor motivation among gifted students seems paradoxical since intrinsic motivation is considered a distinguishing characteristic of gifted students. Renzulli's (1986) definition of giftedness, for example, includes task commitment as a central element. Frasier, Hunsucker, Lee, Finley, et al. (1995) and Frasier, Hunsucker, Lee, Mitchell, et al. (1995) found that teachers frequently cite "keen sense of interest" and "highly motivated" as characteristics of giftedness, their assumption being that interest serves to motivate students. And the most frequently adopted checklist in gifted education has a motivation subscale (Renzulli, Smith, White, Callahan, & Hartman, 1976).

However, not all gifted students are motivated, and many underachieve academically. In a study of gifted Black students, Ford (1995) reported that 38% were underachieving. National estimates are that 20–50% of gifted students underachieve academically (National Commission on Excellence in Education, 1983; Whitmore, 1986). While poor motivation cannot fully account for underachievement, it plays a major role. Many gifted underachievers express a lack of interest in school curricula because they find it uninteresting, meaningless, or irrelevant (Ford; Ford, Grantham, & Harris, 1996). Unfortunately, the referral, screening, and identification process for students will overlook many gifted underachievers, especially if school personnel and parents believe that gifted students are, by definition, highly motivated.

Student Interests and Motivation

An important way to motivate students is to focus on their interests. Interest-based learning is student-centered and increases the likelihood of students being active participants in the learning process. Students have opportunities to focus on topics they consider personally or culturally meaningful and relevant. The most effective learning occurs when students are immersed in an activity in which they can make connections to prior knowledge and interests (Buchanan, Woerner, Bigam, & Cascade, 1997; Dewey, 1965; VanTassel-Baska, 1988; Vygotsky, 1978). Thus, student-centered curricula and instructional activities are guided by the answers to two fundamental questions: How relevant to students, both now and for the future, is the schoolwork they are doing? and How can I use my students' interests to help them learn and to keep them engaged?

Alber and Heward (1996) described "behavior traps" as a way to help develop students' academic and social skills. A behavior trap uses a student's interests to "trap" him or her into using and developing important skills. Effective behavior traps have four essential features:

1. They are "baited" with powerful, virtually irresistible reinforcers that "lure" the student to the trap.
2. Only a small, easy-to-perform response that is already in the student's repertoire is necessary to enter the trap.
3. Once the student is inside the trap, interrelated contingencies of reinforcement motivate the student to acquire, extend, and maintain targeted academic or social skills.
4. They can remain effective over a long period of time because the student shows relatively few, if any, satiation effects. . . . The fundamental nature of behavior traps: easy to enter and difficult to exit. (Alber & Heward, p. 286)

The strategies recommended by Alber and Heward (1996) hold important implications for motivating gifted underachievers. In this chapter, we extend the application of behavior traps to the motivation of gifted students. We provide a rationale for designing plans to motivate students and present several sample motivation traps.

Motivation Traps

Planning, setting, and evaluating motivation traps is a five-step process.

1. Identify which students need help. Which student is struggling? Who is off task? Who seems uninterested, bored, frustrated?

2. Discover what interests students. Who are their heroes? What are their hobbies? How do students spend their leisure time? Students' interests serve as the bait for motivation traps. "Any trap is only as effective as the bait with which it is set. Make an inventory of your students' interests with the intention of using their most zealous preoccupation as irresistible trap bait, like the most delicious cheese for the mousetrap" (Alber & Heward, 1996, p. 286).

    Discovering the most effective bait for motivation traps often requires the least amount of searching. The best bait is usually the most obvious. The more often a student engages in or expresses interest in a topic or activity, the longer the duration of those episodes, and the greater the variety of ways in which the student relates to or engages in the activity, the more likely that topic or activity will be effective bait for a motivation trap. How often does Janna talk about insects? How much time in one sitting does she spend looking at books about insects? Does she draw pictures of insects? Are most of her compositions about insects, regardless of the content of the day's story starter? Does she collect insects? If the answers to these questions are: "Several times each day," "Hours at a time if we let her," "Yes, yes, yes, and yes," then Janna will almost certainly fall "victim" to a well-designed motivation trap baited with materials and activities featuring insects.

3. Find resources and activities to address students' interests. How can I match the topic, lesson, or unit to students' interests? What resources are available? Sometimes, students themselves are the best sources of materials and activities related to their interests.

4. Set the trap. A motivation trap cannot work unless the student gets "caught." Make it easy for students to enter the trap; only a small, easy-to-perform response should be required. Once inside the trap, the student must then use and extend target skills in order to maintain and increase contact with his or her favorite topic or activity. Many underachieving gifted students quickly lose interest in an activity because they are bored by unnecessary repetitions

and impatient to proceed to the next level (Howell, Heward, & Swassing, 1996). Such problems can be prevented by providing gifted students opportunities to participate in activities based on task completion, rather than time schedules. Motivation traps can provide an excellent vehicle to address this need.

5. Evaluate the trap. Few plans remain effective without some type of evaluation. Therefore, it is important to appraise students' successes and failures and consider ways to modify the motivation plan or trap. What was ineffective or effective? How can the trap be improved? Not all students will respond immediately to the trap. Some students will need more time than others. Provide students with substantive feedback on their performance and progress.

For more information and suggestions on designing and setting motivation traps, see Alber and Heward (1996). Sample motivation traps are described in the next section.

Sample Motivation Traps

Hero Traps

Most of us have heroes—famous athletes, movie stars, musicians, authors, and inventors—people we admire and hold in high esteem. Teachers can find ways to incorporate students' heroes as bait for motivation traps in virtually every subject area.

Language Arts. Students can write letters to their heroes. They can write scripts or stories using the heroes as characters, conduct mock interviews of their heroes, read biographies about their heroes, or lead a schoolwide letter-writing campaign to get their heroes to visit their school.

Math. Students can create and compute statistics for their sports hero's accomplishments, such as home runs, batting averages, rebounds, and touchdowns. They can create a budget using their hero's salary.

Content Areas. Students can find the geographic location of their hero's birthplace, concert tours, or sports schedules. They can make a timeline of their hero's career, research the influences and origins of their hero's talent, and make a genealogy chart. Students can produce and direct music videos using their musician hero's recordings.

Fetish Traps

Fetish traps take advantage of a commonly identified characteristic of gifted students: intense interest in a particular topic (Frasier, Hunsucker, Lee, Finley, et al., 1995; Frasier, Hunsucker, Lee, Mitchell, et al., 1995). A fetish trap can be set around just about any topic or activity that a student finds exciting, such as computers, race cars, airplanes, horses, dinosaurs, or bridges.

Language Arts. Have students draw pictures and write stories on their interest. They can write research reports or give oral reports on the interest.

Math. Students can develop important math skills while they classify and compare quantifiable characteristics and performance numbers (e.g., prices, speeds, sizes, weights, duration) of the things they find fascinating.

Content Areas. Students can research the history of their fetish. A student who loves horses might identify and research the past 10 winners of the Kentucky Derby. He or she could write a biography of a female jockey or a Black jockey. Which country was the first to permit a person of color to be in a derby? Why have so few women been jockeys in one country or another? He or she could compare the types and price of horses in Japan versus the U.S.

Classroom Club Traps

Some gifted and talented students tend toward introversion; they may choose to read books instead of actively participating in social, creative, or physical activities (Howell et al., 1996; Silverman, 1995). Encouraging the participation of such students in a classroom club packed with high-interest bait may enable them to extend their social interactions and develop relationships with their peers. Classroom club traps may provide motivation to engage in intellectual pursuits, as well as social interactions.

Once the combined effects of high-interest bait and new friendships have allowed shy gifted students to participate comfortably in a classroom club, the teacher might encourage them to develop leadership skills by having members of the club take turns being the leader. The teacher and students together can generate a list of skills a good leader should demonstrate. Prior to taking over a leadership role in the club, the students can use role-playing to practice skills such as negotiation, teamwork, constructive criticism, and collaborative problem solving. The teacher might begin by stating a problem and having students act out how to solve it (e.g., "What would you say or do if two members of the club disagreed about how to approach a goal?"). Students can practice stating their position or suggestions tactfully and figuring out ways to compromise. The following are a few examples and ideas for classroom club traps.

Cooking Club Trap. Students can apply science concepts (e.g., convection, conduction, boiling points of various substances, chemical interactions), create their own recipes, or publish a cookbook (complete with computer graphics) and sell it as a fundraiser.

Science Club Trap. Students can collect, classify, and inventory their collections of rocks, shells, plants, or insects. They can collaboratively research topics, conduct experiments, and present and publish their findings.

Inventors Club Trap. Students can create their own inventions as possible solutions to problems (e.g., overpopulation, air pollution, diminishing resources) current technology has not addressed or exacerbated.

Classroom Newspaper Trap. Students can conduct interviews, write book and movie reviews, report on school events, write editorials, take and develop their own photographs, and make up riddles, jokes, brain teasers, and puzzles.

Creative Writers Club Trap. Students can write their own fiction, share story ideas, help edit one another's work, and coauthor stories collaboratively.

Sports Trading Card Club Trap. Students can figure out ways to classify players based on their strengths and weaknesses, create new statistics and software for describing and predicting a player's performance, or develop mathematical formulas to project future performances based on athletes' trends, current performance, and age.

Classroom Store Club Trap. Students can figure out how to minimize costs and maximize profits, create advertisements, and test-market new products.

Social and Emotional Needs Traps

Some students underachieve for social and emotional reasons; they want to be accepted, they want attention, they feel isolated, and so forth (Ford, 1996). Other students may resort to off-task or disruptive behaviors to avoid looking incompetent or to hide their uncertainty about a task. Some gifted students, in their attempts to address these social and emotional needs, may assume the role of tattletale, note passer, spitball thrower, airplane thrower, or class clown. For these students, the negative attention their misbehavior produces is better to them than no attention at all. Teachers can sometimes set a motivation trap to turn a student's off-task, disruptive behaviors into on-task, productive behaviors. Following are two examples.

Note-Passing Trap. Reserve a special time each day for students to pass notes to one another. This activity could gradually be expanded into a pen pal club in which students write and reply to letters from people outside the classroom.

Tattletale Trap. Encourage and teach the "tattletale" how to write about the positive behaviors of his or her classmates. Have the student keep a record of important school/classroom events and let him or her read the recorded notes to the class at the end of the school day or week.

Conclusion

Teaching is a hard job when students make an effort to learn. It is an impossible one when students make no effort to learn. It is an unfortunate reality that every classroom will contain at least one unmotivated student. Teachers of gifted students are no exception. Underachievement is a complex phenomenon, and interventions to improve student achievement and motivation can be complicated and time-consuming. Motivation traps provide teachers with one strategy for increasing students' engagement by placing students at the center of the curriculum and requiring teachers to consider their interests, as well as their social and emotional needs. We contend, as do others, that a student-centered curriculum is a critical ingredient if students are to reach their potential in schools. Motivation traps can help students achieve at higher levels by making instructional activities more engaging, relevant, and meaningful.

References

Alber, S. R., & Heward, W. L. (1996). Gotcha! Twenty-five behavior traps guaranteed to extend your students' academic and social skills. *Intervention in School and Clinic, 31*, 285–289.

Buchanan, N., Woerner, B., Bigam, N., & Cascade, C. (1997). Developing talent in high school students: An integrative model. *Roeper Review, 19*, 208–212.

Dewey, J. (1965). *Experience and education.* New York: Collier.

Ford, D. Y. (1995). *A study of achievement and underachievement among gifted, potentially gifted, and average students.* Storrs: The National Research Center on the Gifted and Talented, University of Connecticut.

Ford, D. Y. (1996). *Reversing underachievement among gifted Black students: Promising practices and programs.* New York: Teachers College Press.

Ford, D. Y., Grantham, T. C., & Harris, J. J., III. (1996). Multicultural gifted education: A wake-up call to the profession. *Roeper Review, 19*, 72–78.

Frasier, M. M., Hunsaker, S. L., Lee, J., Finley, V. S., Garcia, J. H., Martin, D., & Frank, E. (1995). *An exploratory study of the effectiveness of the staff development model and the research-based assess-*

ment plan in improving the identification of gifted economically disadvantaged students. Storrs: The National Research Center on the Gifted and Talented, University of Connecticut.

Frasier, M. M., Hunsaker, S. L., Lee, J., Mitchell, S., Cramond, B., Krisel, S., Garcia, J. H., Martin, D., Frank, E., & Finley, V. S. (1995). *Core attributes of giftedness: A foundation for recognizing the gifted potential of minority and economically disadvantaged students.* Storrs: The National Research Center on the Gifted and Talented, University of Connecticut.

Howell, R. D., Heward, W. L., & Swassing, R. H. (1996). Gifted and talented students. In W. L. Heward (Ed.), *Exceptional children: An introduction to special education* (6th ed., pp. 531–583). Englewood Cliffs, NJ: Merrill/Prentice Hall.

National Commission on Excellence in Education. (1983). *A nation at risk: The imperative for educational reform.* Washington, DC: U.S. Department of Education.

Newmann, F. M. (1992). Introduction. In F. M. Newmann (Ed.), *Student engagement and achievement in American society* (pp. 1–10). New York: Teachers College Press.

Renzulli, J. S. (1986). The three-ring conception of giftedness: A developmental model for creative productivity. In R. J. Sternberg & J. E. Davidson (Eds.), *Conceptions of giftedness* (pp. 53–92). New York: Cambridge University Press.

Renzulli, J. S., Smith, L. H., White, A. J., Callahan, C. M., & Hartman, R. K. (1976). *Scales for rating the behavioral characteristics of superior students.* Wetherfield, CT: Creative Learning Press.

Silverman, L. K. (1995). Highly gifted children. In J. L. Genshaft, M. Birely, & C. L. Hollinger (Eds.), *Serving gifted and talented students: A resource for school personnel* (pp. 217–240). Austin, TX: PRO-ED.

VanTassel-Baska, J. (1988). Curriculum design issues in developing a curriculum for the gifted. In J. Van Tassel-Baska, J. Feldhusen, K. Seeley, G. Wheatley, L. Silverman, & W. Foster (Eds.), *Comprehensive curriculum for gifted learners.* (pp. 53–76). Needham Heights, MA: Allyn and Bacon.

Vygotsky, L. S. (1978). *Mind in society.* Cambridge, MA: Harvard University Press.

Whitmore, J. (1986). *Intellectual giftedness in young children: Recognition and development.* New York: Haworth.

Professional Development and School Improvement

chapter 15

Through the Looking Glass
one school's reflections on differentiation

by **Carol Tieso**

eachers approach professional development and in-service opportunities as if they're approaching a train wreck. They know they must see what's ahead, but they can't bear the sight of it. Most teachers recoil in fear when professional development days appear on the school calendar. Further, when allowed a choice, they will generally choose workshops that will add to their "bag of tricks"—brief, hands-on activities they can use in their classrooms on Monday, instead of the sometimes painful specter of initiating long-term, systemic change in their standard operating procedures.

Teachers must deal with a diversity of students' abilities, strengths, and interests in their classrooms while at the same time covering the material, prepping students for standardized tests, and preparing themselves to be "highly qualified." Legislation requiring services for gifted and talented students and the paucity of quality programs for such students has left the classroom teacher to fill the void, which brings up the question: How do classroom teachers address issues of equity and excellence while pursuing curricular and instructional innovations that fundamentally change the way schools operate? Further, how do classroom teachers receive the training they need to teach to students' varying abilities, interests, and learning styles?

There has been one innovation introduced that has demonstrated initial and lasting change: peer or technical coaching (Joyce & Showers, 1995) combined with strategies and techniques for enhancing and differentiating curricula for high-ability students. I had the opportunity to work as a technical coach with an elementary faculty for an entire year. This article represents a summary of that action research study, the purpose of which was to chronicle a year of implementing technical and peer coaching models to help teachers modify, differentiate, and enrich the curriculum for diverse learners.

Technical or Peer Coaching

Over the past 2 decades, Joyce and Showers (1983, 1995) have published the seminal work on technical or peer coaching. They defined *technical coaching* as coaching that occurs with the assistance of a university representative, usually from a school of education, who is fluent in the curricular or instructional innovation they seek to implement. *Peer coaching* is defined by the collegial, collaborative efforts of teaching peers as they implement innovations as a group. Joyce and Showers (1995) also suggested that teachers learn from each other in the process of planning instruction, developing the materials to support it, watching each other work with students, and thinking together about the impact of their behavior on the learning of their students. From their earlier studies they suggested that teachers who had a coaching relationship practiced new skills and strategies more frequently and applied them more appropriately than did their counterparts who worked alone to expand their repertoires. Members of peer-coaching groups exhibited greater long-term retention of new strategies and more appropriate use of new teaching models over time. Coaching helped nearly all the teachers implement new teaching strategies. Equally important, teachers introduced to the new models could coach one another, provided that the teachers continued to receive periodic follow-up in training settings (Showers & Joyce, 1996, p. 14).

Joyce and Showers (1983) also warned of several potential pitfalls that must be avoided when implementing a coaching model. First, teachers need a deep understanding of content and pedagogical skills if they are to institute lasting change. Since many teachers are generalists by nature, many do not have the content-specific skills required to delve more deeply into subject matter. Next, teachers must be prepared to implement innovations immediately after initial training or risk losing the enthusiasm inspired by that training. Further, coaches must be prepared for the rough spots that may impede implementation. The autonomy and solitude of teaching may create a culture resistant to change, even if that change creates a collegial and collaborative work environment. The worst offenders are often the veteran teachers who have a stake in maintaining the status quo and are resistant to trying new methods and ideas. Next, teachers must discuss when to use a strategy in addition to how. Teachers used to reviewing the same curricula can sometimes miss opportunities to introduce new strategies or materials. Finally, teachers must be prepared to fail. That is, they must be prepared to admit that a strategy or method was unsuccessful and move on. Gifted students especially appreciate honesty and sincerity from their teachers and can be quite forgiving. Students also become creatures of habit and may resist initial attempts to change the learning environment. At these times, the support and friendship fostered within the study team is vital to ensuring continued implementation.

If these potential obstacles can be overcome, coaching can be a highly successful staff-development model. The research on technical and peer coaching suggests that an ongoing, supportive team approach is the most successful type of staff-development practices in use today.

Total School Improvement

Renzulli (1994) introduced a model of talent development for all students while providing for the most able among them. One major component is curricular modification, which includes the "triaging" of textbooks (the analysis and surgical removal of unchallenging and repetitive content), modifying existing curricular units through the use of advance organizers, employing higher level questioning strategies, connecting the unit of study to the disciplines, compacting the curriculum (Renzulli, Smith, & Reis, 1982), and designing units of study based on interdisciplinary concepts (Kaplan, 1986; Renzulli, 1988; Renzulli, Leppien, & Hays, 2000).

According to Renzulli (1994), most classroom curriculum development is driven primarily by textbooks, the quality of which has declined substantially in the past 20 years. The reality of large, heterogeneous classes necessitates teaching to the middle, which means that students at either end of the ability spectrum are left behind. Curricular modification frees time for more challenging learning experiences by streamlining and eliminating learned content; thus, teachers have more time to add depth and breadth to the existing curriculum.

A second major aspect of Renzulli's plan for school improvement includes enrichment teaching and learning. This is characterized by Renzulli's (1977) original approach to gifted and talented programming, the Enrichment Triad Model, which consists of Type I enrichment (e.g., general exploratory activities such as guest speakers, field trips, oral presentations); Type II enrichment, which includes group training activities (e.g., methodological and thinking skills); and Type III enrichment, which suggests original individual or small-group investigations of real-world problems.

A third major component of Renzulli's model is curriculum differentiation, which includes the extensive use of preassessment to determine students' strengths, interests, and learning styles; flexible grouping practices that necessitate the creation of small groups based on those preassessed areas; and the differentiation of existing curricula by increasing their breadth (interest, choices, and learning style variation) and depth ("tiering" lessons for different ability levels).

Collegial Coaching in One Setting

I had the opportunity to work as a technical coach with an elementary school faculty for an entire school year to provide training in classroom modification or enhancement, differentiation and enrichment practices, and monthly technical coaching. Two school-level lead teachers (the enrichment teacher and the media specialist) and separate grade-level leaders were chosen prior to my introduction as the technical coach. Each grade-level leader was sent to Confratute, the University of Connecticut's summer institute for enrichment teaching and learning. The teachers were administered a needs assessment (Schlichter & Olenchak, 1992), and I worked with individual grade-level teams monthly over the course of the academic year using Showers and Joyce's (1996) model of technical and peer-coaching study teams. The model suggests that the training components proceed in the following order: theory presentation, modeling or demonstration, guided practice, structured and open-ended feedback, and in-class assistance with transfer. The teachers practiced the strategies and reported back to me on their progress. Additionally, teachers invited me to observe differentiated practices and provide feedback on the lessons. The teachers also provided feedback on any difficulties or obstacles they encountered during the implementation phase. After the initial 1-year technical coaching period, the GT and grade-level lead teachers took responsibility for ongoing peer coaching, procurement of resources and materials, and development of community resource contacts.

The teachers decided to create study teams from each grade level, with two or three teachers on each team. Additionally, the special education teacher and the language arts specialist also sat in on frequent meetings. As students vary in their levels of readiness and ability, so do teachers.

The fourth-grade teachers were immediately prepared to implement advanced differentiation strategies such as tiering assignments because the study team leader, Teacher R, had already completed modification or remodeling of his existing curriculum. He first tried to tier a math lesson, but reported that he was very frustrated with the results. He had one student who had completely mastered the material, and he wondered why there was a need for him to complete any additional work in this area. I suggested to him that this was a case in which curriculum compacting (Renzulli, Smith, & Reis, 1982) might be a more appropriate strategy. The group discussed the mechanics of curriculum compacting, working on the documentation and the replacement activities.

Another fourth-grade and first-year teacher, Teacher M, indicated that she had had trouble with tiering. The group discussed the tiered lesson and realized that she had tried to tier a lesson that was actually a skill that students could either perform or not. They discussed the need to use concepts and principles and other big ideas in order to tier efficiently. At the next meeting, Teacher M reported that the next tiered lesson had been more successful.

Later, the fourth-grade teachers implemented a program of independent projects entitled "Anything Goes." At the end of the yearlong collaboration, Teacher M discussed her learning and growth:

> Two of my boys who did Titanic blew my mind, too. They got all dressed up and did an interview, and the way that they did it was so creative and it really came across. We didn't really do a lot of planning. We know that they spent a lot of time at each other's house after school, but I really didn't know what was going to happen. I think that it was a good experience because the kids felt they could really go for it. And they did.

Teacher M also tried to enrich her curriculum by inviting more guest speakers to her classroom (Type I experiences). She invited her brother to speak to the children about music and opera. An additional positive consequence was that he had been identified with AD/HD and dyslexia as a young man. The students were mesmerized by his theatrical reading and commented about his reading ability. The teacher felt that the students were enlightened and surprised that someone who had been recognized as having a learning disability could be so successful.

Sometimes, strategies that are cognitively powerful also find a voice in the affective domain. Teacher R commented on his awakening to the reality of students' differing learning styles:

> That's a good point because I don't think that, in the past in education, the belief was "Let's work with their

learning styles." It was "Let's make them get this style." And now it's "Let's work with them and evaluate them because you can't change somebody's learning style." It's what it is, so you work with it. And I think in the past people had always tried to change the kids to fit a particular mold.

Teacher J, the special education teacher, also commented that, because she was involved with the entire faculty, she saw pretesting and curriculum compacting being used on a regular basis:

Not only in fourth grade, but I think a lot of the classes are doing a lot of the pretesting to compact. And I'm also seeing that there are different ways to assess the students, and it doesn't have to be the same instrument for everybody to tap into their learning styles. That's been kind of exciting to see.

The first-grade teachers were also a polished group. They already used many of the strategies of modification and differentiation (flexible small groups, modification of the curriculum, and tiering of assignments), so the focus became implementing the Schoolwide Enrichment Model (Renzulli & Reis, 1997). The first-grade teachers had two objectives: (1) create interest centers for reading focused on author studies and nonfiction and (2) develop and implement enrichment clusters (Renzulli, Gentry, & Reis, 2003).

The group used the Total Talent Portfolio (Renzulli & Reis, 1994) and an interest inventory to survey the students' interests. They found that the students' reading interests were *Stellaluna* and the *Nate the Great* series. Other interests included science, African music, and architecture and building. The first set of enrichment clusters was developed from this initial interest information. The clusters ran for 1 hour on 5 consecutive Fridays. Parents and community volunteers were solicited, and some of the groups presented their work at "Thrilling Thursday." A second set of clusters was begun in the spring with an identical format. In a culminating session at the end of the year, the teachers summarized their first experience with enrichment clusters and other aspects of SEM.

Teacher D: The biggest thing we've started has been the enrichment clusters. They've been a huge success, and then doing them again, getting to change a few things, fix some things. We're going to take your suggestions [and look at] assessment, real audience, and real products in the end. That's been wonderful, and the kids really love it; they really look forward to it. I think as far as my centers in the classroom are going, I've expanded my scope of what I do in the classroom. There's one little boy who's really interested in geography. We got these new books, and I've been working with him on topography and map skills. I'm not doing much whole-group instruction anymore. On the one hand, it sort of makes you feel guilty, and on the other hand, you look around the room and see them all very busy and being productive and that's the thing: You want them active and moving around and doing something, rather than listening.

The kindergarten teachers represented an interesting challenge. Because they didn't have any primary teaching experience, I often consulted with them regarding their curriculum. Since many of the strategies of modification and differentiation reflect higher level concepts and principles, this group decided to focus on an integrated unit based on the students' top interest choice, "Pets."

They began their unit with a discussion about what kinds of pets they had at home. They followed up with data collection and the creation of a pictograph describing the class's choices of pets. They then brainstormed potential Type I general exploratory experiences. They decided to invite a dog groomer, a pet store owner, and a veterinarian in as guest speakers. The students were enthralled by the X-rays brought by the veterinarian and were intrigued by the rocks lodged in the dogs' stomachs. That issue gave rise to another brainstorming session with me in which potential group culminating projects were discussed. At the end of the collaboration period, students in Teacher J's kindergarten class surprised me with a fully illustrated, published version of their original story "Rocky, the Rock-Eating Dog." All students in the class contributed to the work—some by their ideas, some by their writing, and some by their illustrations. Late in the school year, the teachers spoke fondly of the unit on pets and of one young girl in particular who couldn't print her letters on her own.

> Teacher J: I always send a little letter welcoming them to school, but this year I just thought I would do a little survey to see what their interests were and maybe go from there. I think with you being here, it kind of pushed me into doing it. [Talking about the "Rocky" picture book], we learned a lot from this book. Of course, we've been writing all year anyway; we do have our own publishing company. [We started with the] character, Rocky, and brainstormed. And that's really how it got rolling. We did not use everything we brainstormed. We had a beginning, middle, and end, but it probably could have been longer because they just went wild with it. Not all the children were able to write, so for one little girl, I held her hand and we did it together.

There were also struggles in this process. Some teachers were advanced in their use of the strategies, while others had trouble just implementing them. The principal was amazed at the progress of some of the teachers who had spent the majority of their careers using whole-group instruction and were now overheard telling parents about their use of flexible grouping and tiered lessons. The principal was especially excited at the progress of the students; she noted that their questions and interest level at school assemblies were at the highest level she had ever noticed.

The most significant outcome was that students perceived that their teachers were utilizing formal and informal preassessment techniques and flexible grouping practices in their daily lessons. Students indicated that they worked in small groups based on interests, learning styles, and abilities. Additionally, they were exposed to different resources and produced different projects for authentic audiences.

Conclusion

Teachers indicated that students at their school perceived that instruction in their classrooms was differentiated based on resources used, type of work completed, activities chosen or assigned, and complexity of work completed. They also indicated that they were differentiating instruction based on interest, learning styles, and ability; were modifying questioning strategies; and, finally, were enriching their curriculum by compacting students out of work already mastered, offering choices and alternative products, and utilizing small, flexible groups based on choice, learning styles, and expectations.

These anecdotes are significant in that they reveal the effectiveness of ongoing and supportive professional development practices. Teachers were encouraged to begin at their own level of readiness and proceed at their own pace. Teachers indicated that they were excited about meeting the needs of some of their brightest students and were open to trying new teaching and grouping strategies. I observed the increased quality, complexity, and sophistication of the students' products and verbal communication. Additionally, students expressed joy at having the opportunity to work at their own pace and in their own interest areas.

As this case study has shown, technical or peer coaching is a professional development model that can successfully and systemically bring change to a school environment. Schools and school districts must make the financial and emotional commitment to further this mode of professional development, especially if teachers are expected to enhance and differentiate their curriculum to meet the needs of students at all ability and readiness levels.

References

Joyce, B., & Showers, B. (1983). The coaching of teaching. *Educational Leadership, 40*(1), 4–16.

Joyce, B., & Showers, B. (1995). *Student achievement through staff development.* White Plains, NY: Longman.

Kaplan, S. N. (1986). The grid: A model to construct differentiated curriculum for the gifted. In J. S. Renzulli (Ed.), *Systems and models for developing programs for the gifted and talented* (pp. 180–193). Mansfield Center, CT: Creative Learning Press.

Renzulli, J. S. (1977). *The enrichment triad model: A guide for developing defensible programs for the gifted and talented.* Mansfield Center, CT: Creative Learning Press.

Renzulli, J. S. (1988). The multiple menu model for developing differentiated curriculum for the gifted and talented. *Gifted Child Quarterly, 36,* 298–309.

Renzulli, J. S. (1994). *Schools for talent development: A practical plan for total school improvement.* Mansfield, CT: Creative Learning Press.

Renzulli, J. S., Gentry, M., & Reis, S. M. (2003). *Enrichment clusters: A practical plan for real-world, student-driven learning.* Mansfield, CT: Creative Learning Press.

Renzulli, J. S., Leppien, J. H., & Hays, T. S. (2000). *The multiple menu model: A practical guide for developing differentiated curriculum.* Mansfield Center, CT: Creative Learning Press.

Renzulli, J. S., & Reis, S. M. (1994). Research related to the schoolwide triad model. *Gifted Child Quarterly, 38,* 7–20.

Renzulli, J. S., & Reis, S. M. (1997). *The schoolwide enrichment model: A comprehensive plan for educational excellence.* Mansfield Center, CT: Creative Learning Press.

Renzulli, J. S., Smith, L., & Reis, S. M. (1982). Curriculum compacting: An essential strategy for working with gifted students. *Elementary School Journal, 82,* 185–194.

Schlichter, C. L., & Olenchak, F. R. (1992). Identification of inservice needs among schoolwide enrichment schools. *Roeper Review, 14,* 159–162.

Showers, B., & Joyce, B. (1996). The evolution of peer coaching. *Educational Leadership, 53*(6), 12–16.

chapter 16

What Gift?

the reality of the student who is gifted and talented in public school classrooms

by **Tempus Fugit Glass**

he era of No Child Left Behind legislation is an excellent time to examine the field of gifted education. Bines (1991) lamented that, after more than 70 years of research, there is not even consensus on an operational definition of giftedness or the most reliable method for identifying gifted students. Evidence does support the following statement: There are some youngsters who are born with the capability to learn faster than others those ideas or concepts that societies value in children and in adults (Baldwin, 1994). According to Dalzell (1998), giftedness may be defined simply as intellectual precocity. Incumbent upon educators remains the challenge to resolve these lingering obstacles in order to best serve the students who are identified as gifted and therefore entitled to gifted education services.

The Nature of Giftedness

One critical factor of gifted development is cognition. Lewis and Michalson (1985) described cognition in gifted individuals as "comprising curiosity, attention and superior memory." Another trait noted in gifted individuals is precocious language development. By the age of 2 or 3, many have extensive vocabularies and use of complex sentence structure. Gifted children also differ from the norm in several other ways: They are highly motivated, extremely independent, and tend to be more introverted and introspective (Winner, 1996). Meador (1996) described gifted children as people with the ability to learn rapidly, having advanced ability in a specific domain such as math or reading, to be creative, and to be verbally proficient.

The Evolution of Giftedness in the U.S.

In order to comprehend the state of affairs faced by gifted students in public schools, it is necessary to understand the history and politics that have brought current policy and practice to where it stands. Prior to the 20th century, accounts of giftedness contained an aura of mystery. Child prodigies were targets of intense scrutiny and were looked at as "freaks of nature" by many, including renowned French psychologist Alfred Binet (Hildreth, 1966). Many educators viewed highly intelligent students as deviants whose exceptional abilities were liabilities, rather than assets (Jost, 1997).

To date, the seminal study of giftedness is Lewis Terman's *Genetic Studies of Genius* (1925), which tracked the lives of more than 1,000 highly intelligent children. The shift in American attitudes toward giftedness began with its publication. Although there are diversity issues associated with this study, namely cultural and economic, Terman's findings are summarized in a 1922 American Psychological Association address, in which he stated that gifted children are "superior to unselected children in physique, health, and social adjustment; [and] marked by superior moral attitudes."

According to Bines (1991), special programs designed to accommodate bright kids have been around since the turn of the century, but the idea of identifying the gifted as a distinct group first gained scientific credibility in the 1920s. The first nationwide push to improve education for gifted students came in the 1950s, the early years of the Cold War. In 1958, Congress approved the first-ever direct federal aid to education: The National Defense and Education Act (Jost, 1997). The goal of educating gifted students took a back seat in the 1960s to concerns about educational equity. The civil rights and anti-poverty movements focused attention on the poor quality of education being provided to youngsters in urban ghettos and centers of rural poverty. The need to educate the brightest competed with a strong egalitarian imperative to provide the best quality education to all students (Tannenbaum, 1993). Improving the schooling of "at-risk" students became the driving force in American education (Renzulli & Reis, 1991). Yet, virtually no parallel emphasis on providing high-end excellence and access for advanced learners existed (Tomlinson, 1994).

In 1970, Congress included a provision in an omnibus aid to education bill calling for the Commissioner of Education to conduct a study on the needs of gifted students. The resulting 1971 report by Commissioner Sidney P. Marland, Jr. depicted gifted students as a neglected minority of at least 2.5 million pupils. The report provided the impetus for the federal government's first direct assistance to gifted education, which came in the form of the Office of the Gifted and Talented, which was housed under the Bureau of Education for the Handicapped. In 1974, Congress appropriated to states the first program of financial aid specifically for gifted students. A follow-up study commissioned by the Office of Education in 1976 reported progress, but concluded that gifted education still suffered from inadequate funding, a shortage of trained personnel, and questionable methods for identifying gifted students (Jost, 1997).

In 1988, Congress approved the Jacob K. Javits Gifted and Talented Student Education Act. To date, the Javits Gifted and Talented Education Program in the U.S. Department of Education remains the federal government's only program designed for the education of gifted students (Jost, 1997). In the past 17 years, there have been no further improvements and no mandate for gifted education at the federal level.

The Identification Dilemma

Historically, children tested with the Stanford-Binet IQ instrument who score 136 or higher have been designated as gifted (Bracy, 1994). The validity of the Stanford-Binet as the criterion to identify gifted individuals has come under serious criticism from those who believe that IQ testing excludes a whole host of other ways in which giftedness can be manifested. Critics of gifted education forcefully complain that students in special academic programs are predominantly White and middle class. The resulting disparities have fueled charges that gifted and talented education often represents little more than privileged education for privileged students at public expense. Such criticism calls into question current procedures and stimulates a search for alternative identification policies (Gallagher, 2000).

Many gifted programs have already deemphasized IQ and achievement tests in favor of more inclusive alternative identification procedures (Frasier, 1991). Texas and Georgia are among the states that have recently adopted guidelines calling on local school systems to use multiple criteria in identifying students for gifted programs. One of the National Association for Gifted Children's guiding principles for identification is that "Instruments used for student assessment to determine eligibility for gifted education services must measure diverse abilities, talents, strengths, and needs" (Landrum, Callahan, & Shaklee, 2001, p. 44).

The Design Dilemma

Debate continues pitting inclusive classroom settings against homogeneous grouping practices. Educational reform efforts stress heterogeneous grouping as a desired practice (Hoekman, McCormick, & Gross, 1999). This inclusive classroom structure consolidates exceptional youngsters in groups with regular students who have different educational needs (Thornton, 1995). It is as members of a regular classroom that gifted students typically receive the majority of their instruction (White, 2000). "The view that gifted students will be able to develop their full potential in an inclusive classroom environment is highly naïve," noted Jost (1997), adding, "gifted students have a tremendous thirst for complexity, which requires additional materials and an accelerated rate of learning. They require a differentiation in the curriculum and instruction so they can maximize their potential."

The lack of challenge in the curriculum for higher level students is exacerbated by public schools when they cope with budgetary shortfalls, increasing enrollment, demands on teacher time, and lack of teacher skill by placing gifted students in regular classrooms with curricula aimed at the abilities of the average pupil (Jost, 1997). Boring, monotonous busywork may also be stressful and demotivating for individuals who prefer higher level thinking and reasoning activities. High-IQ students are able to handle about twice as many challenging tasks as an average-IQ student. A person with great skills, but few opportunities for applying them will ultimately become bored and possibly anxious (Hoekman, McCormick, & Gross, 1999).

According to Thornton (1995), "Our school systems are actually giving tacit approval to creating underachievement in one ability group so that the needs of the other ability group can be served. . . . This . . . is egalitarianism at its worst." In line with this theoretical framework, one of the essential goals for education becomes the provision of a level of challenge beyond the current level of skill (Bloom, 1985). Each individual's full potential is not explored if the majority of the class can complete every task with relative ease (Meador, 1996).

The intellectual potential of gifted students depends, in part, upon optimal educational intervention. It is the duty of the schools to notice precocious children and provide for their education, just as it is the duty of the schools to provide for all others (Piirto, 1999). Public schools move between these two models, but, despite what educational research shows, heterogeneous grouping and cooperative learning approaches appear to have the advantage in policy debates. The Department of Education has estimated that only about 5% of U.S. students are enrolled in gifted classes of some sort. Special classes for the gifted remain the exception, not the rule. Therefore, most gifted kids spend all day in regular classrooms where it is the classroom teacher who bears the responsibility for the majority of instruction for gifted students on a day-to-day basis.

The Bottom Line: Funding

The final, and possibly least discussed, issue at odds with gifted education is funding. Funding for gifted education is meager. Frank Rainey (1996), former director of gifted and talented education in Colorado, commented, "Gifted education in most places is way underfunded at the state level. Considering that there are probably as many gifted kids as there are kids with disabilities, there's a huge difference." The federal government fares little better, spending only $5 million in 1996 on the only educational program targeted specifically at gifted and talented students—less than .02% of the Department of Education's $31 billion budget (Jost, 1997).

Promising Practices and Approaches

No Child Left Behind needs to consider gifted education. Rather than homogeneous teaching of groups of heterogeneous students, educators are increasingly focusing on flexible groupings based on the academic and personal potential of each child. To promote and encourage students, gifted curricula stress high expectations and stimulation, which, when combined with care and support, foster an environment where talents can develop and flourish.

Where does that leave the state of education for gifted students in today's schools? What strategies and applications can we, as educators, use to benefit all students? What promising practices and approaches are being implemented to ensure that we are not wasting a most valuable resource?

One of the most often-presented strategies of educational improvement for gifted students is sophisticated personnel preparation. Teachers of the gifted and talented are given special training, after which they can better prepare individually appropriate curricula and recognize the characteristics of giftedness or high-ability students in their own classrooms.

In addition, the gifted teaching specialty requires the teacher to have further developed skills than his or her regular classroom counterparts. The specialist must possess content sophistication, be able to differentiate lessons and units, and teach complex ideas and conceptualizations. Once content standards are established in general education, the gifted specialist adds to these standards, creating a "standards-plus" criteria that enhances content for gifted students. The key element is to provide a measure of gifted education training to all teachers since every teacher is responsible for educating the gifted students in their own classes.

Another increasingly popular strategy for gifted education programming is maintaining minimum standards of student contact time with gifted education specialists. Including gifted students in the regular classroom is feasible and supported when a gifted specialist comes into the classroom and provides extension opportunities. No consensus exists among educators concerning the amount of time the specialist should spend with the students and their regular teachers. Currently, most of the decisions that determine policy are driven by economics.

The ability grouping model is another useful approach. This model stresses interaction with peers of similar ability levels to decrease frustration and interpersonal isolation. Working with peers of like ability enables gifted children to gain insight into their own abilities. This method also allows teachers to organize classrooms more effectively and accommodate a variety of developmental ranges. Techniques currently in use include grouping for specific subjects, grouping for specific talents, or grouping to provide high-ability students enriched or accelerated curricula. Students who satisfactorily demonstrate mastery of educational objectives are allowed to progress deeper into the subject area by moving above and beyond general competencies toward higher grade-level standards or enrichment opportunities rooted in the course curriculum. Students are also encouraged to take ownership of the process by focusing on areas that hold great personal or group interest.

A centers approach to enrichment activities is also highly effective as a method for expanding upon general curricular requirements. A well-organized center in the regular classroom can provide alternative activities, second-tier activities, or self-guided activities that add depth to the regular curriculum. The center can also provide students an avenue to showcase talents, work at an individualized pace, and personalize educational experiences.

The Current Reality of the Gifted
in Public School Classrooms

One important question to raise in educating gifted students is, "Are current educational practices beneficial, or merely established?" Schools can contribute to problems if they fail to give gifted students an appropriately challenging curriculum. Research-supported practices are only useful if they are implemented. One of the most cherished principles of American education is equality of opportunity. No Child Left Behind cannot, at its core, be interpreted to mean that the brightest students must wait on the slowest. *All* students should have the right to exercise their talents to the fullest potential. Accepting the educational philosophy of excellence for all does not equate to identical education for all. There are no identical students. Why, then, should there exist identical programming? In the realm of education, cookie-cutter models offer no solution.

In this country, the overriding quest for equity has been purchased at the expense of excellence. Without advanced or enriched programs, gifted students may fall short of their potential, or worse, lose interest in school altogether. The goal of educating people to the best of their abilities remains unrealized if all people are not educated at their level. Encouragement alone will not suffice. Children gain self-confidence through intellectual challenge. The key lies in providing a range of activities that allows all students, including the gifted, to display their fullest abilities.

America's brightest young people have quit learning. Since curricula have been "dumbed down" to help weaker students, gifted students perceive no need to work in order to achieve or succeed. This policy often amounts to expecting the brightest students to tutor other youngsters while waiting for their own instruction at the expense of their own educational development.

Recent changes in curricular emphasis, from mastery of content to improving self-esteem, may be damaging to cognitive development, critical thinking, and national test scores. The dramatic decline of Scholastic Assessment Test (SAT) scores from 1963 to 1980 reveals genuine deterioration in the education of our college-bound students. Today, median SAT scores are lower by about 150 points than they were in 1963 (London, 1996).

In addition, our culture maintains ambivalence toward intellectuals. Intellect is not something we revere. Outstanding mental ability is not viewed as a gift. Kids who care passionately about their education many times carry the stigma of being "odd" or "nerds." The truly unthinkable response to this dilemma is to ignore the need for change.

Not to recognize and develop the abilities of gifted and talented students will stifle their opportunity and negate their potential both personally and as contributors to society. How is it possible for someone to give back what he or she never receives? If a gift is to be valued, it must be desirable. Are we creating an environment that creates desire for achievement, success, and excellence, or are we inadvertently modeling a system that holds mediocrity as the ultimate achievement and homogeny as the true ideal? The truth is, individual attention, emphasis on critical thinking, encouragement of potential, high expectations, and enrichment experiences are sound educational practices. Gifted programs have exposed one glaring and encompassing problem: We expect too little from too many. As we move further away from the pursuit of excellence, we come closer to providing little more than "big kid" daycare.

References

Baldwin, V. (1994). The seven plus story: Developing hidden talents among students in socioeconomically disadvantaged environments. *Gifted Child Quarterly, 38,* 80–84.

Bines, J. (1991, December 16). Aren't we special? The dope on "gifted" education. *The New Republic, 205*(25), 16–18.

Bloom, B. (1985). *Developing talent in young people.* New York: Ballantine.

Bracey, G.W. (1994). Finding gifted kids. *Phi Delta Kappan, 76,* 252–255.

Dalzell, H. J. (1998). Giftedness: Infancy to adolescence—A developmental perspective. *Roeper Review, 20,* 259–265.

Frasier, M. (1991). Disadvantaged and culturally diverse gifted students. *Journal for the Education of the Gifted, 14,* 234–245.

Gallagher, J. J. (2000). Unthinkable thoughts: Education of gifted students. *Gifted Child Quarterly, 44,* 5–12.

Hildreth, G. (1966). *Introduction to the gifted.* New York: McGraw-Hill.

Hoekman, K., McCormick, J., & Gross, M. U. M. (1999). The optimal context for gifted students: A preliminary exploration of motivational and affective considerations. *Gifted Child Quarterly, 43,* 170–193.

Jost, K. (1997). Educating gifted students: Are U.S. schools neglecting the brightest young? *CQ Researcher, 7,* 265–268.

Landrum, M. S., Callahan, C. M., & Shaklee, B. D. (Eds.). (2001). *Aiming for excellence: Annotations to the NAGC pre-K–grade 12 gifted program standards.* Waco, TX: Prufrock Press.

Lewis, M., & Michalson, L. (1985). The gifted infant. In J. Freeman (Ed.), *The psychology of gifted children: Perspectives on development and education* (pp. 35–57). New York: Wiley.

London, H. (1996, October 30). Education and the money question. *Washington Times.* (Article ID R00056640105)

Meador, K. (1996). Meeting the needs of young gifted students. *Childhood Education, 73*(1), 6–9.

Piirto, J. (1999). *Talented children and adults: Their development and education* (2nd ed.) Upper Saddle River, NJ: Merrill/Prentice Hall.

Rainey, C. J. (1996). Speech presented to the council of state directors of programs for the gifted. In Council of State Directors of Programs for the Gifted, *The 1996 state of the states gifted and talented education report.* (ERIC Document Reproduction Service No. ED405711)

Renzulli, J. S., & Reis, S. M. (1991). The reform movement and the quiet crisis in gifted education. *Gifted Child Quarterly, 35,* 26–35.

Tannenbaum, A. J. (1993). History of giftedness and gifted education in world perspective. In K. A. Heller, F. J. Mönks, & A. H. Passow (Eds.), *International handbook of research and development of giftedness and talent* (pp. 3–27). Oxford: Pergamon.

Terman, L. M. (1925). *Mental and physical traits of a thousand gifted children: Genetic studies of genius, Vol. 1.* Stanford: Stanford University Press.

Thornton, B. M. (1995). Handicapping our future. *National Review, 47*(18), 64–67.

Tomlinson, C. A. (1994). Gifted learners too: A possible dream? *Educational Leadership, 52*(4), 68–69.

White, D. A. (2000). Gifted students and philosophy: The sound of a tree falling in the forest. *Gifted Child Today, 23*(4), 28–33.

Winner, E. (1996). *Gifted children: Myths and realities.* New York: BasicBooks.

chapter 17

The Application of an Individual Professional Development Plan to Gifted Education

by **Frances A. Karnes** *and* **Elizabeth Shaunessy**

esearch indicates that ongoing, high-quality staff development is essential to achieving significant standards-based reform (Sparks, 2002). Currently, the majority of teachers do not regularly participate in staff development practices in the United States (Richardson, 2002). Staff development decisions have traditionally been made by school administrators to meet the needs of students and to address school, district, and national goals in gifted education. In this model, teachers have been sideline observers with little or no participation in the planning of these professional development efforts. While this paradigm is cost- and time-efficient, this one-size-fits-all approach to staff development fails to address the learning needs of each teacher in a district (Richardson).

Recently, however, the concept of individual professional development plans has emerged as a way to involve teachers in the decision making and goal setting of professional development (Collins, 1997; Guskey, 1999; Richardson, 2001, 2002; Sparks & Hirsh, 1997). This model gives teachers the opportunity to learn more about the needs of their students, their own learning needs, and how these align with district goals and national standards. Teachers reflect about how students learn in their classes based on student grades, attitudes, or other information. Educators then formulate questions they would like to pursue, develop an individual learning plan centered on their guiding questions, execute the learning plan, document accomplishments, assess the effectiveness of the plan, reflect on their learning process, and repeat the process (see Figure 17.1).

Such individualized professional development plans allow educators to set their own goals and increase the likelihood that intended results will be achieved (National Staff Development Council, 2002). Rather than a single event, long-term professional development supports ongoing change and challenges teachers to be lifelong learners, designing plans with specific purposes aimed at intended learning (Wetherill, Burton, Calhoun, & Thomas, 2001/2002).

Many districts are beginning to recognize that all teachers can benefit from designing individual professional development plans (Richardson, 2002). District leaders encourage the professional growth of their teachers through these plans that link "individual learning with school goals and schoolwide learning with district goals" (p. 1). Furthermore, several districts that have required individual professional development plans for their teachers have received the U.S. Department of Education's Model Professional Development Awards for their outstanding staff development activities. All teachers, regardless of subject area or grade level, can grow professionally through this process and can positively affect student learning, including teachers who already demonstrate excellence in their teaching.

Components of the Professional Development Plan

The individually developed learning plan has implications for professional development in gifted education. Using information about the performance of gifted children, attitudes of gifted children and their parents, and classroom practices can help teachers identify potential areas of professional growth. Based on this information, teachers can address learning goals in the development of their individualized professional development plans.

The components of a professional development plan in gifted education should have the following characteristics: personal information and professional responsibilities, a goal statement of the plan, objectives, activities, the intended impact on the students, a timeline, and a means for evaluation. The relationship to district and state goals for the gifted should also be specified.

The individual completing a professional development plan in gifted education should state what the proposed results would be. Sharing the information with an appropriate audience is the last step of the process.

Ways to Accomplish the Plan

There are many ways to accomplish an individual professional development plan beyond the traditional staff development. Karnes and Lewis (1996) suggested the use of specific videotapes with brief descriptions of each. Videos provide easy access to professionals in the field of gifted education without the high cost of transportation, consultant fees, lodging, and food.

Shaunessy and Karnes (2002) offered ideas for additional professional development standards beyond those set forth by the National Association for Gifted Children (NAGC). One of these standards focuses on the ease of access to professional literature. They presented a broad list of journals in the field, along with a basic listing of professional books, including those for regular education teachers working with the gifted and those in specialized programs.

A variety of collaborative efforts between teachers has also shown positive learning results for teachers and students. Collins (1997) recommended two types of collegial learning activities: peer coaching and joint work. In peer coaching, teachers observe other teachers in order to reinforce prior training in a specific methodology or strategy. The shared experience extends the training through "application and analysis in the classroom" (Collins, p. 95). The process is experimental, allow-

Name _____

Address _____

Phone (school/home) _____ E-mail _____

Teacher in Regular Classroom _____ Grade(s) _____

Teacher in Specialized Program _____ Grade(s) _____

Counselor _____ Grade(s) _____

Curriculum Developer _____ Grade(s) _____

School _____ Area(s) _____

Administrator _____ Area(s) _____

1.   How did you identify your goal in gifted education?
I recognized that my students may have some weaknesses in leadership based on their classroom actions and their performance on the LSI.

2.   How does your goal relate to improving student achievement?
Students can gain self-confidence, organizational skills, and improved communication skills through the development of leadership skills.

3.   How does your goal relate to district goals for gifted education?
In order to become more skilled in communication and to develop personal learning habits to promote lifelong learning, leadership skills were selected as a targeted area for use in all subject areas. Furthermore, the district goal of promoting student service to the community is one aspect of leadership development through leadership plans designed by each student.

4.   How does your goal relate to the gifted education goals (outcomes) of the student?
Students involved in leadership development gain knowledge in interpersonal skills, communication skills, organizational skills, and intrapersonal skills, each of which is critical to the development of the student as an independent, lifelong learner.

Accomplishments

5.   What data/product will you submit to indicate what has been accomplished?
Comparison of pre and post LSI results, anecdotal records from observations, student products (to include leadership plans, pictures of students executing leadership plans in their school, community, or religious affiliation), comments from parents, and student reflections about their growth as leaders.

6.   When will you present this information to an appropriate audience and in what format? *Results will be shared with school faculty, the PTA, local newspapers (student work, not personally identifiable information). I will also generate an article about my experience to share with other educators and submit to a publication targeting teachers of my grade level and subject.*

Signature _____ Date _____

Figure 17.1. Individual professional development plan in gifted education

Objective	Activities	How will this impact student learning?	Timeline	Evaluation
1. Measure student knowledge of leadership skills.	Use a preassessment, such as The Leadership Skills Inventory (LSI; Karnes & Chauvin, 2000b).	Will allow the teacher to evaluate students' skill levels and design appropriate instruction based on the diagnosis from the LSI.	Quarter 1	Students self-score the LSI and teacher makes instructional decisions based on the pretest results.
2. Note student performance in leadership skills.	Observation	Note how students manifest leadership skills in daily classroom situations to supplement data from LSI.	Quarter 1	Teacher compares observation notes with results from LSI to generate appropriate lessons and activities for students to develop leadership skills.
3. Based on results of preassessment and observation, research how to address student needs.	Consult The Leadership Development Program (Karnes & Chauvin, 2000a) and professional journals and texts pertaining to educating gifted children, specifically in leadership skills. Attend conferences and workshops to learn more about facilitating leadership skills.		Quarter 2	Teacher locates relevant research from most current literature in leadership and gifted education.
4. Develop lessons that incorporate ideas from research related to student needs.	Review literature findings and student data to formulate appropriate activities for leadership development.	Students will receive instruction based on research-based practices. Lessons will not duplicate what students' already know; lessons will address areas of needed development.	Quarter 2–3	Lessons show evidence of suggestions from research and are based on student data from LSI observations.
5. Measure student knowledge of leadership skills.	Use postassessment (LSI).	It will establish the effectiveness of the intervention.	Quarter 3	LSI is again used so that consistency in measurement is used.
6. Evaluate areas of progress and see where additional efforts need to be concentrated.	Compare preassessment with postassessment results. Conduct observations of leadership skills evidenced by students.	New lessons can be generated that will continue to focus on skill weaknesses based on data from LSI.	Quarter 4	New lessons include careful consideration of second LSI administration and student performance.

ing a safe environment and attitude toward trial and error, which is expected in the learning phase of a new practice. Research indicates that teachers involved in peer coaching are able to transfer and apply new skills to a variety of educational situations and retain skills and new knowledge longer than those not involved in such collaboration. Similarly, joint work between educators allows for collaboration at a deeper level; teachers share in "multiple aspects of teaching, such as planning, problem solving, curriculum development, and assessment of student progress" (Collins, p. 104).

Study groups are another option for executing professional development plans with shared goals (Murphy, 1992). Educators work in groups of six or less to discuss central issues, plan units, research learning methods, voice concerns, and learn from each other.

Mentoring also offers educators a vehicle to achieving their professional development goals. A successful mentorship program paired practicing scientists and mathematicians with secondary science and math teachers, resulting in improved teaching skills, increased teacher self-respect, and increased motivation among participating teachers (Miller, 1989). Similar efforts have also been undertaken within the schools between master teachers and novice teachers (Rice, 1987). As in the peer coaching method, teachers observe each other teaching, have time to reflect on the targeted skill, and have the opportunity to reinforce new concepts and sharpen skills.

Web-based and online courses are another venue for teachers to accomplish professional development goals. Professional organizations, educational institutions, and state agencies are increasing their professional development opportunities in widely accessible electronic classrooms, replete with visuals, discussion groups, and tutorials (Apple Learning Professional Development, 2002; Association for Supervision and Curriculum Development, 2002; Council for Exceptional Children, 2002; iEARN, 2002; Tapped In, 2002).

Colleges and universities also offer several formats for professional development activities. Web-based courses, classes, seminars, lectures, professional conferences, and university faculty consultants are ideal ways to maximize a district's access to resources at a local university or college.

Incentives

Dettmer and Landrum (1998) offered many ideas for incentives to participate in staff development, and some have direct application to the creation, implementation, and evaluation of an annual plan in gifted education. School personnel should be given choices of incentives such as graduate credit, increments on a salary schedule, in-service equivalency credit, a sabbatical, a stipend, release time from professional responsibilities, certification renewal, and a substitute to fulfill professional responsibilities while teachers are engaged in the implementation of the plan.

Conclusion

An individual professional development plan is a tool that fosters specialized learning for educators. Results-based staff development that is framed around the personal learning goals of each district educator increases the likelihood that teachers will investigate topics that reflect their students' needs and will have application in the classroom. Individualized learning plans create authentic learning opportunities tailored to the unique needs of each educator, rather than a one-size-fits-all plan for everyone on staff. Proponents of gifted education can use this tool as a means of assisting educators in identifying their needs in terms of educating gifted students within their classes. Data-driven, teacher-selected, goal-oriented individual professional learning plans can ultimately have a significant impact on the learning of gifted students.

References

Apple Learning Professional Development. (2002). *Online courses.* Retrieved May 13, 2004, from http://ali.apple.com/nshelp/welcome.htm

Association for Supervision and Curriculum Development. (2002). *Professional development online.* Retrieved on May 13, 2004, from http://www.ascd.org/trainingopportunities/pdonline.html

Collins, D. (1997). *Achieving your vision of professional development.* Greensboro: SERVE, University of North Carolina at Greensboro.

Council for Exceptional Children. (2002). *Professional development training & events.* Retrieved May 13, 2004, from http://www.cec. sped.org/pd

Dettmer, P., & Landrum, M. (1998). *Staff development: The key to effective gifted education programs.* Waco, TX: Prufrock Press.

Guskey, T. R. (1999). *Evaluating professional development.* Thousand Oaks, CA: Corwin Press.

iEARN. (2002). *Online teacher training to integrate an iEARN collaborative project into your classroom.* Retrieved May 13, 2004, from http://www.iearn.org/professional/online.html

Karnes, F. A., & Chauvin, J. C. (2000a). *The leadership development program.* Scottsdale, AZ: Great Potential Press.

Karnes, F. A., & Chauvin, J. C. (2000b). *The leadership skills inventory.* Scottsdale, AZ: Great Potential Press.

Karnes, F. A., & Lewis, J. (1996). Staff development through videotapes in gifted education, *Roeper Review, 19,* 106–107.

Miller, L. (1989). Mentorships and the perceived educational payoffs. *Phi Delta Kappan, 70 ,* 465–467.

Murphy, C. (1992). Study groups foster schoolwide learning. *Educational Leadership, 50*(3), 71–74.

National Staff Development Council. (2002). *Create your own learning plan: By your own design* [Computer software]. Columbus, OH: Eisenhower National Clearinghouse.

Rice, K. (1987). *Empowering teachers: A search for professional autonomy.* (ERIC Document Reproduction Service Number ED282845)

Richardson, J. (2001, December/January). Support system: School improvement plans work best when staff learning is included. [Electronic version]. *Tools for Schools.* Retrieved May 13, 2004, from http://www.nsdc.org/library/publications/tools/tools12-00rich.cfm

Richardson, J. (2002, February/March). Reach for the stars: Individual learning plans allow teachers to take charge of their own learning. *Tools for Schools,* 1–2.

Shaunessy, E., & Karnes, F. A. (2002). Expanding the national professional development standards in gifted education. *Gifted Education Communicator, 33*(1), 28–29, 36.

Sparks, D. (2002). Dreaming all that we might realize [Electronic version]. *ENC Focus,* 9(1). Retrieved May 13, 2004, from http://www.enc.org/features/focus/archive/pd/document.shtm?input=FOC-002595-index,00.shtm

Sparks, D., & Hirsh, S. (1997). *A new vision for staff development.* Alexandria, VA: Association for Supervision and Curriculum Development.

Tapped In. (2002). *Tapped In calendar.* Retrieved May 12, 2004, from http://ti2.sri.com/tappedin/do/CalendarAction?

Wetherill, K., Burton, G., Calhoun, D., & Thomas, C. (2001/2002). Redefining professional career development in the twenty-first century: A systemic approach. *High School Journal, 85*(2), 54–66.

About the Authors

Sheila R. Alber is an assistant professor of special education at The University of Southern Mississippi. Her research interests focus on generalization and maintenance of academic and social skills.

Linda Garris Christian is a professor of education at Adams State College in Alamosa, Colorado. Her experiences in Head Start, kindergarten, university preschools, and private day care have served her well in her work with early childhood professionals around the country. While her primary research interests are in the area of family and identity development, she has also explored career aspirations of rural youth, stress-management strategies, and cross-generational relationships.

Hazel J. Feldhusen is a former teacher of gifted students who has been studying classroom structure to facilitate the education of gifted students in regular inclusive classrooms.

John F. Feldhusen is a professor emeritus at Purdue University. He has been conducting research with gifted students in grades 2–12 on how well they can identify their own special talents and how they use that knowledge in setting. educational and career goals. The project also seeks to determine how many and how much gifted youth set very high level and creative goals.

Donna Y. Ford is Betts Chair of Education and Human Development at Peabody College, Vanderbilt University. Her work focuses on gifted diverse students, urban education, and multicultural curriculum. She has written several books and articles and consults with school districts nationally.

William L. Heward is professor of special education at The Ohio State University, where he has taught since 1975. His research interests focus on increasing the effectiveness of group instruction in diverse classrooms, improving the academic achievement of students with disabilities, and promoting the generalization and maintenance of newly learned skills.

Earl S. Hishinuma is an associate professor and vice chair of research in the Department of Psychiatry, John A. Burns School of Medicine, University of Hawaii at Manoa. He currently conducts research on issues related to adolescent mental health and education.

Barbara Hoover-Schultz is a gifted facilitator in the Department of Gifted and Talented Education in the Omaha Public Schools.

Andrew P. Johnson is professor and chair of the Department of Educational Studies: Special Populations at Minnesota State University, Mankato. He specializes in holistic education, spiritual intelligence, literacy instruction, action research, strategies for inclusive classrooms, and gifted education.

Frances A. Karnes is a professor of special education and director of the Frances A. Karnes Center for Gifted Studies at The University of Southern Mississippi.

Laura Magner teaches K–3 gifted resource classes at Minor Elementary School in Lilburn, Georgia.

Danna Garrison May is a teacher of gifted fourth-grade students in Petal, Mississippi.

Laura E. McGrail has been a certified school psychologist since 1986. She currently holds the position of head school psychologist/grants coordinator for Henderson County Schools, Henderson, Kentucky. Mrs. McGrail was named the Kentucky School Psychologist of the Year (1995) and National School Psychologist of the Year (1996) by the National Assocation of School Psychologists. Her professional interests include autism, program/grants development, child abuse prevention, and literacy in addition to gifted education.

Steffi Pugh is a gifted support teacher at Tredyffrin/Easttown Middle School in Berwyn, Pennsylvania, and also serves as a gifted liaison to the Pennsylvania Department of Education.

Vickie Randall has taught at the elementary, high school, and college levels.

Elizabeth Shaunessy is the coordinator of the Gifted Education Program and an assistant professor at the University of South Florida. Her research interests include diverse populations of the gifted, public policy in gifted education, and professional development of teachers of the gifted.

Kenneth Smith is the director of enrichment and technology at Sunset Ridge School District 29 and the author of several short stories for children.

Peggy Snowden is in her 29th year of teaching, with experience in elementary regular education, gifted and talented education, and university-level teaching. She currently teaches in the Department of Literacy Education at Plattsburgh State University.

Kevin Teno serves as P-K–8 principal at Shelby County Catholic School in Harlan, Iowa.

Carol L Tieso is an assistant professor in gifted education at the University of Alabama. Her research interests include the impact of flexible grouping and curriculum differentiation models on students' achievement and addressing the social and emotional needs of gifted, talented, and creative students.

Michele Weitz is a middle school language arts and social studies teacher at Sunset Ridge School District 29.

Vicki Whibley is a classroom teacher in Rotorua, New Zealand.